HERE ON THE COAST

HERE on THE COAST

Reflections from the Rainbelt

HOWARD WHITE

HARBOUR PUBLISHING

HARBOUR PUBLISHING CO. LTD.
P.O. BOX 219, MADEIRA PARK, BC, V0N 2H0
www.harbourpublishing.com

Cover painting by Walter J. Phillips
Illustrations by Kim LaFave
Cover design by Anna Comfort O'Keeffe
Text design by Teresa Karbashewski
Printed and bound in Canada
Printed on FSC-certified paper

Harbour Publishing acknowledges the support of the Canada Council for the Arts, the Government of Canada, and the Province of British Columbia through the BC Arts Council.

Library and Archives Canada Cataloguing in Publication
Title: Here on the Coast : reflections from the Rainbelt / Howard White.
Other titles: Reflections from the Rainbelt
Names: White, Howard, 1945- author.
Identifiers: Canadiana (print) 20200393421 | Canadiana (ebook) 20200393650 | ISBN 9781550179248 (softcover) | ISBN 9781550179255 (EPUB)
Subjects: LCSH: White, Howard, 1945-—Anecdotes. | LCSH: Sunshine Coast (B.C.)—History—Anecdotes. | LCSH: Sunshine Coast (B.C.)—Social life and customs—Anecdotes. | LCSH: Sunshine Coast (B.C.)— Biography—Anecdotes. | LCGFT: Anecdotes.
Classification: LCC FC3845.S95 W54 2021 | DDC 971.1/31—dc23

For Mary

Contents

III.
On These Accordioned Shores

IV.
Nothing Can Be Too Big of a Deal If It's Happening Here

V.
Scientifically Enlarging the Facts

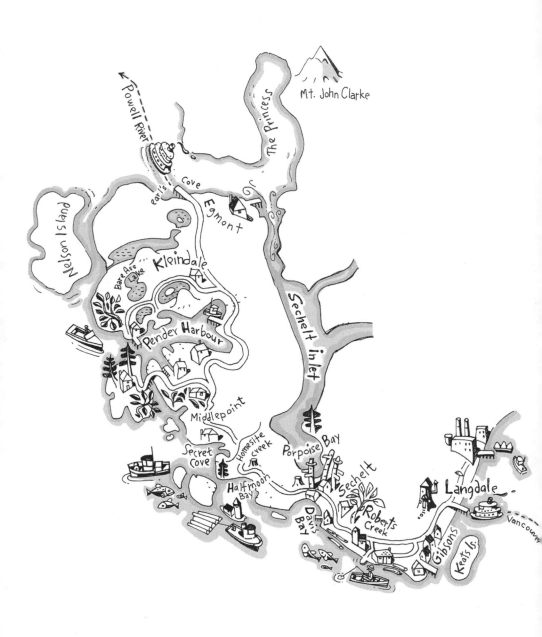

The "Sunshine" Coast

Sunshine on the Raincoast

Off the top I should warn readers that when somebody on the Sunshine Coast of British Columbia says "here on the coast," they don't mean the whole west coast of the Americas or even the whole wet part of BC. They mean just this speck of Pacific shore where they and their close neighbours live, a hundred-mile slab of barnacle-studded granite stretching from Port Mellon to Powell River.

It can be confusing because everywhere on the BC coast, locals speak the same way. When folks out on the west coast of Vancouver Island say "here on the coast," they mean just the surf-pounded stretch from Port Renfrew to Cape Scott, not any of the protected shores along the Inside Passage, which they view as a stagnant backwater not deserving the name *coast*. Same with folks up Prince Rupert way. They think the only coast worthy of the name is their area, where you really have to know how to survive in a desolate watery jungle devoid of fuel docks or radio reception and full of menacing reefs, most unmarked and some even uncharted, where a greenhorn southerner who predictably knocks the leg off their unseaworthy bathtub toy of a boat might go weeks without being rescued by a real coast type from the northern area.

Despite these factional divides, BC coast people are joined by certain things universal to the region: a weary resignation to living with rain and BC Ferries, a familiarity with gumboots, bumbershoots, rain slicks, life jackets, seagull droppings, barnacle lacerations, antifouling paint, disappearing fish, disappearing forests and politics that swing from hard left to hard right never pausing in the middle. To that extent my *Here on the Coast* can be taken as applying to all of BC's salty side, if not extending a bit up and down into coastal America. But in the tradition of attempting to find the universe in a grain of granitic sand, these musings will mainly concern themselves with that portion of the coast that has become known, somewhat absurdly, as the Sunshine Coast.

It took a lot of gall to nickname a piece of certified rainforest "the Sunshine Coast." The blame for that usually goes to Harry Roberts, the pioneer who put Roberts Creek on the map in the early 1900s. He got the idea from his mother, Granny Roberts, who used to tease her neighbours in nearby Gibsons Landing by pointing out that it didn't rain or snow near as much in Roberts Creek as it did in Gibsons. And this is true. It is a proven fact Roberts Creek gets less rain than its neighbour eight kilometres to the south. About three-quarters of an inch less per year. But they both get thoroughly soaked from October to July, just like the rest of this temperate rainforest.

That didn't stop Harry, who had a lot of P.T. Barnum in him, from going down to the Roberts Creek steamboat dock circa 1930 and painting foot-high letters proclaiming THE SUNSHINE BELT on the seaward side of the freight shed. To give him credit, he didn't mean it to be taken seriously. He was just trying to twit the folks around the corner in Gibsons. He blames a "young fellow in the real estate office down in Gibsons" for getting carried away and extending the misnomer to cover the whole coast from Port Mellon to Egmont and trying to fool the world into thinking there was actually some truth to it.

It's funny how well his hoax worked. I have had letters from as far away as Vladivostok congratulating me on living in such a balmy climate. We get travellers showing up here all months of the year in sandals and sunglasses.

There was no Indigenous name for the Sunshine Coast, probably because it was divided between three nations who didn't view it as one territory. The Squamish held the southern end including Gibsons and Roberts Creek; the Sechelt or shíshálh people held the middle section from Roberts Creek to Jervis Inlet; and the Sliammon (or Tla'amin) held the northern section from Jervis Inlet to Desolation Sound. The biggest settlement in the territory was at Pender Harbour, the tiny village where I've lived for the past sixty-five years. The shíshálh name for Pender Harbour was *kalpilin* and they called it that for untold centuries. It has only been called Pender Harbour for less than two centuries, having been renamed on something of a whim by an explorer who probably didn't spend twenty-four hours in the place.

It has gone downhill ever since. There are about three thousand people here now, though it is sometimes hard to believe because the convoluted character of the shoreline does such a good job of concealing the homes. But three hundred years ago there were at least twice as many people living here during the winter months. Every nook and cranny was dotted with longhouses, and the biggest one was reputedly three hundred feet long and six of our storeys high. This was the one called *kla-uhn-uhk-ahwt* and you might say it was the Capitol or Parthenon of the Sechelt Nation. *kalpilin* in those days was one of the great trading centres of the coast—the whole west coast, from the Columbia River to Alaska. Sechelt was just a summer encampment and Gibsons an unimportant satellite village of the Squamish. Here in Pender we still consider Sechelt and Gibsons to be upstart, flash-in-the-pan kind of places that should be more respectful of our elder status, but sometimes our elected representatives have trouble making the rest of the Sunshine Coast understand this.

Getting back to whether or not the Sunshine Coast is quite a legitimate name for a place that gets 1,250 millimetres of rain a year, I want to make it clear that I personally have done what I could to set the record straight. Back in 1972 when my wife Mary and I sat down at our kitchen table on Francis Peninsula to create a journal that would tell the true story of life here on this coast, we decided to call it *"Rain*coast" Chronicles. We believe in truth in advertising. And it must have struck a chord, at least among people who live here and love it for what it is, because *Raincoast Chronicles* has kept publishing for four decades now, adding that neologism *raincoast* to the BC lexicon, to be invoked by anyone who wants to bestow a name that sounds authentically coastal on a boat, book distribution firm or line of pricey party crackers.

Meanwhile the successors of that young fellow in the Gibsons real estate office have been more than busy holding up their end, getting the gag moniker "Sunshine Coast" incorporated into no end of official applications, including the federal riding of West Vancouver–Sunshine Coast–Sea to Sky Country and the Sunshine Coast Regional District. I can hear Harry Roberts chortling in his grave.

I.

A Non-Place on the Map

Getting to Know Us

For much of its life the Sunshine Coast has been a non-place on the map of BC. If you were in Vancouver and said you were from Gibsons or Sechelt, people would assume you were from "the Island," meaning Vancouver Island. If you said you were from Pender Harbour, they would assume you were from Pender Island, which is 240 kilometres away and a whole different kettle of fish. It's only lately the TV weatherpersons have begun to include the Sunshine Coast in their catalogue of BC regions, and they have a pretty loose notion of just where this seldom sunny place is. Lately, they take it to be synonymous with Powell River, which most people on the original Sunshine Coast consider a recent (and not legitimate) claimant to the title. TV news often mixes Powell River and Sechelt in with weather reports for Squamish, which nobody but them has ever considered to be part of the Sunshine Coast.

People who live here are used to living with this kind of geographical confusion. We don't get shirty about it. We're endlessly patient in explaining over and over just where it is that we live. We accept our fate as the regional equivalent of Togo or Dagestan. At least the oldtimers do. After all, most of them came here to get away from it all, so these daily confirmations of anonymity sit okay with them. They had seen the known world and were glad to be out of it.

As a descendant of one of these oldtimers, I didn't share that comfortable opinion. Coming from a noplace made me feel like a nobody, and I vowed I'd take the first chance to get away to a someplace and become a somebody. As far as I can tell, every other kid around me felt the same way, and most of them made good on at least the first part of their vow—to clear out at the first chance. I don't know what happened to me. I got sidetracked. But it helped me to understand when my own kids streaked off to Toronto and New York barely out of their teens.

Now that it's too late to do me any good, there are definite signs that the Sunshine Coast is finally being discovered. I'm not sure I like it. You can get used to being a nobody from nowhere after sixty-odd years of it. I try to think of some advantages of having a slightly higher profile. It is a convenience not having to carry around a pocket map of BC in order to illustrate where you live. It is vaguely interesting to know that the old homestead where I grew up, and was ashamed of, is now appraised at roughly what it cost to build the Lions Gate Bridge. Too bad Dad turned down a chance to buy it for $1,500 back in 1955.

As the oldtimers could have told us, it is not a very long leap from being discovered by the outside world to being taken over by it. It used to be that when you lined up for your Sunshine Breakfast on the 8:20 from Langdale, you could count on being on a first-name basis with either the guy ahead of you or the one behind you. Now there are days you can read your *BC BookWorld* all the way across and not be interrupted once. I swear there are even days I don't know half the people in the noon lineup at the local post office. It seems like the more the world gets to know us, the less we know ourselves.

Fishy Business

"How's the fishing up there?" When I was a kid in the fifties and sixties that would be the most common question when you were in Vancouver and said you were from the Sunshine Coast. If an outsider had heard of the Sunshine Coast at all, chances are they'd heard it was a good place to fish. It wasn't much, but it was something.

I was never interested in the fine points of the piscatorial pursuits but anybody who lived here any length of time could fake a fish conversation without half trying. You could say fishing was great pretty much any time, and never be far wrong. If you wanted to set the hook and play them a little, you could say, "Well, there's a lot of grilse right now but you can get clear of them with a six-ounce weight," or "The bluebacks will be coming in any time now," or "The northerns should be showing up in the next week or so." You didn't have to be part of the in-crowd to know such things; you only had to know the date because the fish runs in those days were as regular as clockwork.

And fishing *was* great. I hesitate to admit it, but I remember one 24th of May when we were having the rellies over, my dad and his pal spent an afternoon bobbing around off Martin Island with a case of beer and caught thirty of those tender little immature coho called bluebacks. I guess you'd go to jail for that now, but there were no limits then. Every evening you would see a flock of kickers out mooching for spring salmon in the "hole" a mere stone's throw off the main steamer dock at Irvines Landing. There was no need to go outside the actual harbour.

First you'd toss out a jig consisting of a short, light line festooned with barbless hooks. This was to catch a few herring for bait, which never took more than a couple minutes. You'd pick the friskiest-looking herring, spear it on a treble hook, lower it to the bottom, reel it up a few turns and wait. If you had to wait more than fifteen or twenty minutes you were having a bad day. Once I didn't have to wait at all; as soon as I dropped my jig over the side I hooked a herring and it was immediately swallowed by a twenty-three-pound spring salmon. Somehow I got the tangled mess of hooks, leaders and fish safely into the boat.

There were times even in those days when you went a whole hour without a bite. In that case, you'd putt out to Temple Rock, drop a cod jig and inside of five minutes the line would be thrumming with a fat big red snapper. You didn't show it off, though. You carried it home in a sack and hoped nobody asked what you had, because mere cod was poverty food. What I'd give for one of those tasty devils now!

I can remember the panic that struck the chamber of commerce types sometime along about the eighties when it became clear the fabulous sport fishing was coming to an end. The thinking was that if outsiders couldn't be guaranteed easy boatloads of fish there would be nothing at all to attract them to this area. The outside world would forget us entirely and all the motels would go broke. The few who suggested this area had a few other attributes that people might still come to enjoy were dismissed as impractical dreamers.

Funny how we could have been so wrong. Outsiders did eventually stop asking about the fishing, but they did find some other interests. Now it's "How are the property values up there?"

What's in a Name?

There oughta be a law against some of the place names that we get stuck with to satisfy the vainglorious whims of land developers. For instance, I live on a road called Rondeview. It was named in the sixties by a developer named Ron, and I guess it was his idea of clever pun. I curse him every time I have to tell a caller, "No, not *Rendezvous*. R-o-n-d-e-v-i-e-w." Someday when I have time I plan to get up a petition to change it to something less embarrassing. My preference would be Whisky Slough Road because I've always admired that flavourful home-brewed place name for the bay down front. Or another time-honoured name for this area, Hardscratch. But I reckon either would be a hard sell with the present-day landowners. Probably Valueview or Investmentcrest would go over better. Anything but R-o-n-d-e-v-i-e-w.

Sunshine Coast place names have always been a bit of a fraud. Except for the original ones, of course, like Sechelt, Sakinaw and Tuwanek, but few of those made it onto official maps. When the first European explorers reached the Sunshine Coast, every nook and cranny had been named by the folks who'd spent several thousand years getting to know the place, the Squamish and Sechelt. Gibsons was *Chekwelp*, Wilson Creek was *Tsawcome* and Pender Harbour, *kalpilin*, but that meant nothing to the visitors. Officers of the British and Spanish navies, they took it as their right and duty to immediately set about renaming the place with words from their own lexicons. It was a prodigious task and setting aside the bald-faced effrontery of it, you have to give these poorly educated mariners credit for the sheer volume of monikers they were able to spew up on short notice.

The first one through the Inside Passage was Captain Vancouver, and he had it fairly easy since he got to name the major features after major figures—the Gulf of Georgia after King George, Howe Sound and Nelson Island after great naval heroes, etc., although by the time he had reached the top end of the Sunshine Coast he was getting sufficiently befuddled he saddled one of the most charming locales on the coast with the lugubrious name of Desolation Sound. It is speculated his gout was acting up on that day.

Later Royal Navy surveyors charged with the finicky business of naming each tiny islet and cove soon ran out of shipmates, wives, sisters, mistresses and pets to commemorate. Captain Richards, who did detailed charting of the Sunshine Coast in 1860, stooped to borrowing names from the racetrack. He was a betting man apparently, and just as he was passing Halfmoon Bay he received a dispatch from Old Blighty containing good news about his wager on that year's Epsom Derby. In his euphoria, he named every feature he sighted that day after some aspect of the 1860 Epsom Derby, including Merry Island, Buccaneer Bay, Tattenham Ledge, Welcome Pass, Oaks Point, Surrey Islands, Epsom Point, Derby Point and, not least, Thormanby Islands after the winning steed. Richards must have had a sense of humour. One of the popular canards about Nelson was that when his higher-ups signalled him to retreat during the Battle of Copenhagen, Nelson put his telescope to his blind eye and said, "I don't see a thing," and fought on to glorious victory. When it fell to Richards to name the large bay entered by a narrow pass on the west side of Nelson Island, he chose "Blind Bay" and "Telescope Passage."

It no more deterred him than it did Rondeview Ron that there were other, less frivolous names well established in local usage that would have served better. Perhaps it's time we took our revenge on some of these name-giving chauvinists by engaging in some judicious revisionism. There has been surprisingly little of this, given the current rage for reconciliation with First Nations. The Haida managed to get the former Queen Charlotte Islands formally renamed Haida Gwaii, and there has been a fairly successful effort to establish "Salish Sea" as a new name for the integrated system of waters comprising Juan de Fuca Strait, Puget Sound and Georgia Strait.

The funny thing about that name "Salish Sea," which many well-intended non-Aboriginals now apply to every bay and backwater on the south coast, is that it was never intended to replace existing names, only to be used when collectively invoking the whole of Juan de Fuca Strait, Puget Sound, Georgia Strait and all associated waters in the lee of Vancouver Island. Also it seems the renamers forgot to consult coastal First Nations on whether or not they would consider "Salish" an entirely appropriate handle for their great inland sea, which it is not. The name "Salish" or *Séliš* originated far from the ocean in the parched badlands of Montana, where it was the chosen name of the Indigenous nation American authorities in their wisdom renamed "Flatheads." These folks lived in quiggly holes rather than longhouses and preferred the taste of fresh buffalo to salmon. "Salish" only came to be applied to the peoples of the coast when non-Indigenous scholars in distant ivory towers decided that the several dozen First Nations occupying the south coast and interior of BC as well as Montana, Idaho and Washington State all belonged to the same Salishan linguistic family, an obscure academic concept on par with saying that Spanish, French and Italian are all part of the Romance linguistic family. Being linked at all was news to the nations involved, who thought of themselves as proudly distinct.

I well remember the Sechelt elder Clarence Joe raging against being lumped together with the Kw'amutsun, who he considered to be traditional enemies. Using "Salish" when one means Sechelt, Okanagan or Lummi is like using "Romanic" when one means Brazilian, Mauritian or Walloon. Better to be a bit more specific.

Mostly, restoration of Indigenous names has been limited to eliminating blatantly racist examples like "Squaw Lake," although one of the most prominent offenders, the famous Vancouver photo spot called "Siwash Rock," remains curiously untouched. Officialdom seems more committed to an indirect campaign of displaying Indigenous place names on road signs in smaller print below the newcomer names, no doubt hoping the originals might catch on. Alas, any chance of this happening is defeated by the practice of spelling Indigenous names using a scholarly spelling system that employs backward question marks, numerals, pointy brackets, Greek letters and other mystifying hieroglyphics such that "Squamish" becomes "Sḵwx̱wú7mesh." This is not an Indigenous way of writing. It is a scholarly writing system called Americanist notation or NAPA. There is nothing particularly Salish about it. I have seen it used in the UK to translate their road signs into unintelligible versions of Gaelic and Welsh. I have never understood how language revivalists hope to bring dying tongues back into popular usage by spelling them in an alphabet that can only be deciphered by those with a degree in linguistics. The Sechelt people, or at least the pointy-headed white guy who originally helped them document their language, devised a special alphabet that mostly avoided upside-down question marks, although it doesn't subscribe to the notion of capitalization. Thus "Sechelt" becomes "shíshálh." I am sure there is a very good argument in support of this grammatical oddity, but I don't know what it is. Neither, I suspect, do most of the shíshálh people.

kalpilin is what the shíshálh people called my hometown and they called it that for hundreds if not thousands of years. It has only been called Pender Harbour since Captain Richards overnighted here in 1860 and named it after his Royal Navy buddy Dan Pender. I would be willing to give up Pender Harbour for *kalpilin* any time. I wonder how Gibsonians like the sound of *Chekwelp*?

Since publishing an earlier version of this diatribe, the shíshálh have called my bluff by formally proposing to change the name of my home neighbourhood, Madeira Park, to *salalus*. Actually I would be sorry to lose the pretty Madeira name, which honours the founder of modern Pender Harbour, but I would be happy to offer a trade for Rondeview!

A Tough Time for Trees

It's a tough time for trees here on the Sunshine Coast. There's the clearcut up in the Chapman Creek watershed, which most of us will never see, though we may eat bits of it when we down a glass of that foggy-looking water. Then there's the great swatches of forest that are getting mowed down to make room for new subdivisions, which does significantly de-green the part of the landscape we move through. But the ones that hurt most are the ones we have around our homes providing shade and privacy, serving as hotels for squirrels and birds and offering sturdy limbs to anchor swings and treehouses. These are the trees we get to know as individuals, almost as family. You see them in old pictures when the kids were small and before the house had been re-sided, looking just the same, providing a reassuring thread of continuity through changing times, just as they've done for hundreds of years. You get attached to them. Plus we now know that it takes one hundred square metres of forest to neutralize the carbon emitted annually by a single car, which makes every tree the more precious.

But the past several years of freakishly high winds have brought a lot of these old friends down across people's roofs, and even the sturdiest-looking specimens have come under suspicion. And falling isn't the only hazard being looked at in a new climate-change light. Anybody who thought the fire hazard presented by trees standing too close to houses was something only communities in dry Interior forests need worry about got their eyes opened in 2019 when Sunshine Coast rainforests began exploding all around us after a record dry spring. Fortunately, midsummer brought enough rain to dampen things down, but only a fool would bet against the dry weather returning, and the BC Forest Service is recommending a tree-free zone of thirty-three feet around buildings.

We had a beautiful cedar about four feet through standing between our place and the neighbour's that suddenly became a point of contention. Their arborist said it was a disaster waiting to happen, while our arborist said it didn't pose any more risk than any other tree and that's what insurance is for. What sealed the old tree's fate was my neighbour saying it kept them up on windy nights, driving the kids to huddle in the farthest corner of the house. That triggered a memory.

Back in the 1950s our family home had a big old grandmother cedar in the front yard that probably could have neutralized the emissions from a school bus just by itself, but we didn't know about global warming then and my dad probably would have given it the chop except that it had a hard lean out over Francis Peninsula Road and not even the best faller could set it down without taking out the power lines. The only solution was to deconstruct it bit by bit from the top down, but the only people who did that in those days were BC Electric and Dad reckoned he would leave it to them. It had such a hard lean away from the house that it didn't appear to pose any risk to us. Still, when the wind blew, we thought about that tree. It was hard to ignore because it had a schoolmarm in it and when it swayed it squawked.

I shared the upstairs bedroom with my kid brother, who was about six, and this one windy night the tree was squawking so loud he got scared and crawled in with me. I told him there was nothing to worry about, given the direction of lean, etc., but I was only half convinced myself. The storm kept rising and the schoolmarm kept squawking louder. There would be a long, drawn out *squee-eee-eeek*, then a pause as the tree reached the perigee of its swing toward us, then a long *squaaa-aaa-aawk* as it swung away toward the road. You couldn't help holding your breath during that pause at the end of the *squee-eee-eeek*, waiting for the reassuring *squaaa-aaa-aawk* that signified it wasn't coming right down on top of us. I was in the midst of recounting the physics of the situation and telling myself I was silly to be so scared when one *squee-eee-eeek* was punctuated by some loud cracks and *whump!* the ceiling of our bedroom crunched down, pinning us to the bed.

Physics be damned, the old tree had fallen straight backward against the lean and taken out the back half of our roof. Apart from being terrified, we were none the worse for wear and actually enjoyed considerable celebrity when the *Coast News* reported the incident the next week. Dad rebuilt the roof using wood from the tree and bought a nice little Austin with the insurance money, so we actually came out ahead on the deal.

But that's the dang trouble with trees. You just never know. There's always the chance of a freak gust that will strike them from an angle they're not braced for, and this hasn't just started happening in the last couple winters. In the latest old cedar question, I had been hanging tough with an offer to top it so it couldn't reach the neighbour's roof, but the idea of scared kids huddling in their beds got to me. I gave in and let them take the old beauty down.

But I think of it every time I open the door, and I think of all the other fine old trees that are getting whacked down along the coast, either as falling or fire hazards. You can hear a steady chorus of powersaws.

Zero Gardening

Starting was always the strongest point of my gardening. Follow-through was my downfall. By August my gardens were always a ruin of weeds. I will say, though, that the weeds inside my garden were always healthier and handsomer than the weeds anywhere else in the neighbourhood, which gave me a twisted satisfaction. This placed me in a good way to appreciate the fashion for gardening with native plants that came to the fore a few years ago. Not only were native plants truer to our own place and time, these new-wave xeriscapers preached, but they grew naturally without the help of polluting fertilizers and wasteful amounts of water.

This seemed like a kind of gardening suited to my natural talents and there was a plot in front of our office that seemed a perfect place to put it into practice. It had been occupied by a large cedar tree the previous owner had cut down, leaving a handsome stump with a sprig of huckleberry just starting to grow out of it. Around the base was a small clump of the plant old-time gardeners like my mother considered their greatest natural enemy—salal. Nothing in the rainforest plant community is harder to dig out and nothing is as determined to re-invade any clear space wrested from its wiry grasp. The sight of it made my hands itch for a mattock, even as my soul filled with despairing conviction all resistance was ultimately futile. But now this formidable foe was in my corner! Nothing in fact was held in higher esteem by the new zero gardeners, who even published instructions on how to artificially introduce salal to areas where it was not already smothering every other form of growth. My enthusiasm for this new kind of gardening swelled.

The question was, what was left for me to add to this already happy little ecosystem? Well, the assemblage was not very colourful, unless you were into infinite shades of green. I decided something from the warm end of the spectrum would look good. There was a considerable patch of crab grass and mint that wanted replacing, so I dug up a wild rose bush and inserted it a safe distance from the salal. That would add a splash of redness in the early part of the summer. For later, I considered foxglove, but the native gardening website denounced that ubiquitous plant as a non-native usurper. Fireweed was sanctioned, so I went to a burnt-over slash I knew to be covered in fireweed in July and sleuthed out a few brownish remains I figured might be fireweed roots and tucked them next to the roses. For blues I visited the cutbank along the Langdale bypass, where I remembered a carpet of lupines, and after digging for about two hours, I excavated a couple of massive roots. It seemed like every lupine on that hill was connected. On the way home I collected about two hundred dried-up pearly everlasting plants from various stretches of roadside and placed them in all the remaining spaces as a neutral backdrop to set off all my bright colours.

This was a lot harder than blowing by Canadian Tire with my Visa card unsheathed, but I consoled myself with the thought that once I had the stuff in the ground, I would never have to touch it again. Then I waited. And waited. By July it was clear none of my transplants had taken, except a few spindly and shocked-looking pearlies. So I cheated and went out and collected some fireweeds, lupines and tiger lilies that were thriving in their natural settings and transplanted them on the go as it were. This drew compliments for about a week, whereupon they wilted and fell over. I gathered some more, telling myself I was actually engaging in a sophisticated kind of planting, since these mature plants would ultimately scatter their seeds over my plot, begetting rich growth the next year. Not.

The next spring my plot was full of promising little shoots that turned into either crab grass or mint. I did realize a little plant I had overlooked the first year was turning into quite a handsome Oregon grape, and there were some small sword ferns emerging from roots that the previous tenant probably thought he had eradicated. But nary a hint of anything not green. The salal grew a bit fuller and began choking out the one plant that did produce a little redness, the huckleberry.

I invested in a weighty tome called *Gardening with Native Plants* by one Arthur Kruckeberg and tried again, carefully assessing soil types and light conditions, but still no dice. Meanwhile the salal expanded, the Oregon grape sent up three new heads and the sword ferns unfolded like green umbrellas. It occurred to me this little plot of west coast nature had a mind of its own and I was only getting in its way. Five years later the whole area is a dense, green mass of salal, Oregon grape and sword fern. It's natural. It's healthy. It requires no human intervention whatever. My only problem is getting passers-by to understand that this apparently wild clump of brush is a carefully planned horticultural event. I have been considering planting a little sign, but can't come up with quite the right wording.

The Electric Diary

I greatly admire these folks who produce a New Year's letter detailing all the wonderful things they managed to cram into the last twelvemonth. I never read one without getting inspired to do one myself, but after sitting in front of a blank screen for ten minutes unable to think of a single thing worth mentioning to my suddenly hypercritical circle of acquaintances, I give it up, thoroughly depressed at the apparent barrenness of my existence. This is where it used to be useful to have a diary—you could flip through the entries and reassure yourself that your life was in fact much more eventful than feeble memory allows—but who has had time for a diary since they were fourteen?

Well, folks, I am not just here to deepen your blues, I am here to announce a solution. Technology to the rescue.

I discovered it by accident. It works like this. Last Christmas, Mary picked up on some subtle hints and bought me my own personal smart phone. Yes, I realize I am about a decade late with this but it had taken me years to master all the hidden features of my flip phone and I was loath to just cast all that hard-won knowledge away. It seems to be a tenet of the digital age that the moment ordinary folk begin to get comfortable with any device or program, it's time to declare that product obsolete, stop supporting it and force everyone to adopt a new version where all the familiar functions are hidden in inconvenient new places. I was holding out against this pernicious trend, but eventually decided being able to get Instagram pictures of the new grandbaby at all hours of the day would be worth it. I asked for the cheapest one available, with an eye to keeping the guilt factor to a minimum if I should lose it or wreck it, because my plan was to keep it in my jacket pocket so I'd always have it in case I found myself on the scene of another Dziekanski tasering or at least of someone going under the table at the office Christmas party.

I promptly forgot about this ambition and left the phone at home most of the time but, it turns out, not all the time. Not having figured out how to sort the various outings into separate "albums" the way the (incomprehensible) manual recommends, my entire year's shooting is jammed pell-mell into one giant file in my computer's My Pictures directory, and through some crossing of virtual wires I find myself watching this entire file run past my eyes in "Slide Show" mode.

There's the bunch from the office down at Baker's Beach for an after-work swim last July. Now, in the inky depths of winter it seems almost impossible to imagine swimming outdoors, let alone having enough sunlight to do it after work! What was that cute co-op student's name, anyway? Now here's a scene I was trying to forget: one I took for insurance purposes showing the charred rubble that was all that remained of our rental house after it burned at the end of last year. Was that a mere year ago? Funny how the big traumas seem further away than they are. There's that chubby three-point buck who kept our grapevine so nicely trimmed all summer. I wonder whose freezer he's in right now? Whoever it is, I hope they appreciate the fine grapey aftertaste. There's friend Anna with her trousers rolled up wading through that funny landlocked tidepool we discovered up at the head of Hotham Sound last August, proof we got at least a little boating in this year. And here's the going-away party for our prized editorial prodigy Emma, leaving the coast to start a new life closer to civilization and eligible bachelors. The year was not without its touching moments, now that I think of it. And speaking of that, here's sweet Callan, our brand new grandson, squinting at the light on his first day of life. That alone is enough to make this a year among years. Now here's a nice one—it's spouse Mary, sitting with my 101-year-old dad and his 98-year-old bride Edith in their sunny September garden, their late-life love preserved for all time.

The random images flow on, kindling memory. And to think, this absorbing pageant is but a tiny fragment of all that really did happen, a few random samples from the times I actually remembered to take the phone, and to occasionally raise it up and click. It gives me a new appreciation of all that can happen in a single year, a year that I couldn't think up anything to say for just an hour ago.

It's a great cure for the January blues. This year I'm going to take twice as many pictures and call it my photo diary. Maybe I can even turn it into a bestselling book: *Photo-Therapy: How to Click Your Way to a New Appreciation of Everyday Life*. Try it. I recommend it.

The Boating Life

I am standing on my head covered in a greasy substance that smells like the innards of a very old hockey bag, so it must be spring.

Aw, the boating life!

I am located in the bilge of our family pride and joy, a thirty-year-old modified fishboat, with one leg kinked painfully around the battery box and the other hyperextended over the exhaust manifold fumbling in icy cold water trying to figure out why the automatic water pump has ceased being automatic.

As seems unavoidable at such times, I begin calculating the number of boat-hours I spend doing things like this, adding it to the time I will spend crawling underneath the hull on the beaching grid with my gumboots full of mud and copper paint running into my armpit, adding it to the time spent making midnight excursions in the midst of winter storms to check tie-up ropes, and dividing the sum total of all this misery into the hours actually spent out on the water enjoying summer sunshine. I know better than to start along this line of figuring because for years now, the answer has been a negative number that just gets more negative each year as the boat and I both get older.

Oddly, and I guess this is what marks me as a true pleasure boater, I never allow the cruel facts to in any way undermine my dedication to the notion of owning a boat.

I don't have to, because my wife Mary takes care of this for me. She is fond of pointing out that—just in terms of annual cash outlay spent hauling and painting, replacing corroded wiring, R-and-R'ing alternators, new and bigger inverters, two-way fridges and occasionally new, more powerful engines the boys justify in terms of reduced exhaust emissions—it would be far more cost-effective to charter a brand new fifty-foot SonShip for two weeks each July. There would probably even be money left over to hire a couple paid crew and a professional chef. She might even deign to come along if I did that. Best of all, we would actually be forced to take two weeks off and use a rental while we had it, instead of the usual "not this week, maybe next" that fritters away our summers under the owned-boat system.

In my defence I must point out I am not by any means alone in my folly. Think of those seventy-foot, four-storey jobs you see at the Seattle Yacht Club outstation in Garden Bay. Those babies not only cost millions to buy in the first place, their fuel consumption is on par with that of a Boeing 737. I find it difficult to conceive of the income you'd need to be able to have spare room in it for one of those floating pleasure domes. Our boat may be a hole in the water into which we dribble our few hard-earned dollars; those things are veritable fortune-sucking maelstroms. How damn rich must these people be? And look how many of them there are! You can go down to the Reed Point Marina in Port Moody or the Sidney Marina on Vancouver Island and cast your gaze over a vast prairie of gleaming fibreglass and chrome. The value of pleasure craft tied up at dock on any given day of the year in BC must be in the billions. And those favoured folks don't seem to get much more use out of their dreamboats than I do out of my old fishboat. You can go down to the Vancouver Yacht Club wharf (well, you can't really get past the razor wire, but you can study it from Canada Place with field glasses) and even in the prime cruising days of August you will see most of that multi-billion-dollar fleet still tied up, depreciating a million dollars a minute waiting for the owners to spare a few days from their frenzied getting and spending.

Pleasure-boat owning has to be the hands-down worst investment in the world.

I know this.

Last year I didn't get out on the *Lisa Diane* for more than one longish weekend. We set sail from Bargain Harbour on Friday intending to go to Desolation Sound to visit a friend who was writing a book there (it takes a work tie-in to pry us loose these days) but a southeaster came up and blew us into Blind Bay. Anna tried to jig up a cod for supper without success and the anchor dragged so I didn't sleep. On Saturday the wind let up enough for us to sneak over into Hotham Sound where we poked around eating salmonberries, worrying about grizzly bears and wading in that pretty but frigid tidal pool up by the head. It rained a lot. On Sunday we returned to port a day early and that was it for the year.

But you know what? Those three days were such a tonic I have been daydreaming about them all winter. Eight months later it is still a favourite lunchroom topic among those who made the trip. It was one of the high points of the entire year.

Something sharp is jabbing my left thigh, causing me to writhe in the grips of a muscle cramp. But I don't care how miserable I feel down here in this cold bilge. Even for one more truncated trip like last year's, I will consider myself well repaid.

Confessions of a Home Handyman

My intentions were the best. That nobody can deny. Our office used to have a dishwasher, back when it was a house. There was a hole for it. The pipes were still dangling from the wall. Then a working dishwasher became surplus when my wife decided to update hers for one of the new environmentally friendly models—I argued that environmentally friendly dishwashers are like environmentally friendly SUVs, but I didn't expect to win that one—so I decided to surprise the staff by installing the surplus one in the office.

I don't know why, but washing coffee cups in our office was at that time one of those tasks that seemed to be beyond our organizational abilities. In their regular roles our staff did the work of companies three times our size, but show them a coffee cup in need of rinsing and they just kind of went pale and staggered away groaning. I had tried everything to convince people they could rise to this challenge, to no avail. Now it occurred to me a nicely broken-in GE Potscrubber would solve one of the great miseries at the heart of our work experience and guarantee me hero status for at least a week.

I dragged the beast up the stairs to the lunchroom one evening and, lying on my back and kicking with both legs, bullied it into the old hole. Everything lined up just like it was meant to.

I like to think of myself as handier than the average couch

potato. I can join up wires with those little plastic dunce-cap thingies. I don't really know how a dishwasher works, but I can figure out that the big hose goes on the big pipe and the little one goes on the little. Even when it came to the plastic pressure fittings with several little bits inside, I managed to put them together without anything left over. I fired the relic up and checked for drips. Perfectly dry. I loaded it with week-old cups and soup bowls with concretized food in them, filled the soap holder and set the dial at extra-heavy duty. And went away.

But there was something bothering me. I couldn't quite figure out what it was, but it bothered me all night. It was still bothering me in the morning, so I went down to the office early to see if I could figure out what it was.

When I opened the door to the ground-level floor, I had an odd sensation. The atmosphere was like, like—a swimming pool. Chlorine in the air. And I could hear water splashing. I stepped into the main room where all the copiers and printers are, and sank into ankle-deep water. I looked down the hallway past all the offices and it was ankle-deep all the way. The stairs to the upper floor where the lunchroom is were now the site of a very picturesque waterfall.

Then it came to me: maybe it would have been better to do the trial dishwasher load in the daytime when you could keep an eye on it. Just in case I'd guessed wrong about which way the bevel was supposed to face on one of those bits in the pressure fitting ...

It is hard to say what was worst, the shock of realizing what I had done, the ignominy of explaining just how this disaster had come about to my unamused colleagues, the three miserable months of working under sheets of plastic with drywall dust raining down on our heads, or getting the bill for $20,000. I'm willing to call it a tie.

At least I got to find out what restorers do. My restorer was a jolly fellow who made me feel much better by telling me how many others shared my misfortune. He had thirteen dishwasher malfunctions on the go at that very moment, including one at the home of my next-door neighbour, who had lost a newly installed hardwood floor for his pains. He seemed so sympathetic I decided to take him into my confidence and confess I felt like a bit of a fool over the way my handiwork worked out.

"Oh, we love do-it-yourselfers!" he said with a chuckle. "You keep us in business." Somehow that left me feeling not so good again.

The only good thing that came out of it was that people have completely stopped asking me to fix things around the office. And remarkably, I haven't seen a sink load of dirty dishes for months. I may have finally got my message across.

Climate Talk

Back in 2006 my friends at the office gave me a little Christmas gift consisting of one of those insulated mugs with a plastic slot you can put your own message in. Mine had the message I SURVIVED THE STORMS OF '06. The slogan seemed apt at the time because 2006 had been one of the worst years up to that time for winter windstorms and we'd spent almost two weeks without power, spread over half a dozen outages. This was when people first began to be aware something was going on with the weather and there was panicky scare talk that climate change might be coming true a lot faster than we thought. Up until that time I used to kind of laugh when the lights went out. It happened so rarely it brought a welcome shakeup of daily routine.

But this morning the lights blinked and here I was cursing at the top of my lungs. This has gone beyond a joke. I've had it with camp-stove coffee and trying to work in the cold with one flickering light bulb, the computer losing its memory every time the generator skips a beat. As a novelty it was tolerable, but as a way of life—it's the pits.

This morning the lights come back on after five minutes— probably just the guys fixing some jury-rig they put up during the last outage—but you can't help wondering, what happened to that sense of approaching apocalypse we all had when the current run of extreme weather events first started hitting home? More than a decade on, people have stopped talking in such an alarmed way about climate calamities like worst-in-a century flooding, all-time record wildfires and windstorms that have caused a 265 per cent increase in power outages in the past four years according to BC Hydro. But it's hard to get much of a conversation going about that. It's become a worn-out topic, like Donald Trump's millionth lie.

Back in '06, official BC seemed content to treat that very bad weather year as a one-off. The Vancouver Park Board left one section of the Stanley Park blowdown on the ground as a memorial to that year's storms, as if never expecting to see the like again. The government used the same kind of thinking on the mountain pine beetle outbreak that destroyed much of what remains of BC's merchantable timber. The plan has been to clear off all the diseased trees and plant exactly the same species in their place, as if the slowly warming trend that spawned the beetle plague will end any day now and things will normalize over the next eighty years.

Whether you accept the consensus of scientific opinion that changing weather patterns are the result of global warming caused by human pollution or whether you side with the Fraser Institute claim this is just a natural shift like others we've had in the past, there is no longer any denying that a shift it is, so we better adjust to it. The Vancouver Park Board should redesign Stanley Park assuming that storms like those of '06 will be the norm rather than the exception for the foreseeable future. The Ministry of Forests should replant the old lodgepole pine stands with species that can survive warmer winters. And here on the Sunshine Coast, BC Hydro better hire back some of the line crews they laid off over the past fifteen years. But is any of this happening? Year after year the government drastically underestimates the amount they put in the budget to fight wildfires, as if a return to the levels of the 1960s can be expected going forward. And the regular folks who were momentarily panicked by these increasingly scary weather events back in 2006? Rather than becoming ever more concerned, we have become tired of talking about it. Yeah, yeah, another flood in Grand Forks. Those people should just move to higher ground. BC's world-class glaciers melting much faster than expected? Yawn. We are becoming inured to natural disaster. This may be an even more dangerous attitude than outright climate change denial.

Talking Hard Times

Dr. Nouriel Roubini, a.k.a. "Dr. Doom," the economist who predicted the 2008 financial crisis and the coronavirus financial crisis (though not coronavirus itself), is still steadfastly predicting harder times ahead. Some might point out even a broken clock is right twice a day, but I think I might be genetically susceptible to such predictions because I find them impossible to ignore.

Even if you want to face this kind of scary music, though, what do you do? The portfolio managers of course will keep up their chorus of "Don't panic. Stay the course. Have faith in value. Over the long haul, we'll all make our 10 per cent." Well, a company called MacMillan Bloedel was once considered the epitome of value. It was the colossus of BC industries with huge pulp mills at Nanaimo, Port Alberni and Powell River. Whatever happened to it, anyway? Now Harmac is being operated by staff, Powell River is limping along on one cylinder and they seem to change the name over the mill gate every few months. What the hell kind of a name is Catalyst, anyway? It sounds more like a pyramid vitamin scheme than a respectable forest products company. Westinghouse was once considered an unassailable bastion of value. So were the Alberta oil sands.

My late father used to rub his hands with glee when he heard Dr. Roubini's kind of talk. "I think people are in for a big surprise," he'd chortle. "All the signs remind me of 1929. Runaway speculation on Wall Street. Everybody playing the stock market. Plants shutting. The president telling us we've never had it so good, despite more poverty and homelessness than ever. Do you know Herbert Hoover and R.B. Bennett kept saying that right through the darkest days of the Depression? Oh yes, I can feel it in the air. This one is going to make the dirty thirties look like a picnic. I'm glad I won't be around."

The good news is that my poppa had been sensing this air of impending financial doom to varying degrees for as long as I can remember, going back to the late 1940s. Once he had me so worried I actually converted my life savings into three tiny gold bars, which promptly lost 50 per cent in value. I wonder if they're still under that loose brick in the fireplace? Sooner or later I guess he'll be proven right, but in the meantime he spent his adult life missing out on the greatest growth cycle in the history of the world. I used to point out to him that if he'd put that $1,500 into the Lougheed property instead of a rusty backhoe back in 1956, he could have sat on his butt and made more money than he did working like a fiend for the following four decades. Not only would he have been able to live in luxury for the rest of his days, so would I.

What intrigues me is the notion that there ought to be something you could invest in that would have good value now, and wouldn't lose it if things do get as tough as the pessimists predict. A good little farm, maybe. Buy the land, get some keen young organic couple to run it, sell the produce locally, watch the value grow as food scarcities increase. No matter what happens, you've still got a chunk of property, and you can always feed yourself. Keeping to the food theme but being more coast-appropriate, a shellfish farm might do the trick. Or if you couldn't afford that, how about starting a small herd of omega-3 pigs? The only fly in this oinkment is every farmer I know, wet or dry, wants to bail out to escape the hard work and thin margins.

A woodlot, perchance? Trees grow with very little outside help. But wood is one of those commodities that doesn't fare well in recessions. And it's tough eating. How about some kind of low-tech survival gear that would be in demand if broad supply networks broke down? Wind mills? Pelton wheels? Hand tools? Another of my dad's strategies dating back to his gyppo logger days was to lay in a good supply of junk. Old truck wheels, chunks of rusty pipe, bed frames, washing machine motors, Model T axles, gearboxes, every kind of engine part. His back yard was a popular stopping place for the area's handymen even in good times, and would have been a gold mine if Canadian Tire ever shut down. Too bad he gave in to neighbourhood outrage and dunged it out.

I am aware this list of depression-proof investment strategies is less than compelling, but I still think the idea has promise. Watch for some trendspotter like Malcolm Gladwell to come out with a bestseller on the subject, thereby securing his own economic future.

My friend Jerry had another approach to making sure he would get full value from his stash that was guaranteed to work. His plan was to move into as nice a condo as he could find, go on as many cruises, take as many plane trips to exotic climes and indulge in as many enjoyable habits as he could while he still could. If I brought up the prospect of an unprovided-for future he'd say, "At least I'll have a great bunch of memories in the bank, which is more than you'll have." He tottered into his grave a couple years back with an empty bank account and a big smile on his face. Much as I envied him, I can't bring myself to follow his example. Like most, I will probably go on doing exactly as the financial advisers and authority figures advise. And that's probably a good thing.

II.

The Only Chance These Things Will Ever Have to Be in a Book

The Great Getaway

When not contemplating economic collapse and worrying about spending winters barricaded in the basement with fifty cases of canned beans, the mind returns to its usual preoccupation for the back end of the year, namely snowbirding.

It has to be admitted, the most popular winter activity on the lovely Sunshine Coast is getting the heck away from the place. If you walk down the main street of Puerto Vallarta or Melaque in January the chances are better than even that you will meet a neighbour, or at least someone you recognize from the chow lineup on the *Queen of Surrey*. And it isn't only realtors and motel owners anymore—now you're just as likely to run into the scruffy dude who delivers your firewood, taking full advantage of Mexico's tolerant attitude toward public drinking and urination.

Exactly why all and sundry feel such a need to escape our rather wimpy winter may not be obvious to the outside observer. Even the odd five-day power outage doesn't get us much sympathy from Ontarians and Maritimers fighting the blizzards and ice storms of the Real Canadian Winter. The excuse I find most satisfying is seasonal affective disorder (SAD). It enlists science to show those long grey months of soggy skies, mild though they be, are actually as bad for your health as avalanches and ice dams. Maybe worse. The more dramatic type of winter event makes for scary television, but it passes quickly and leaves survivors stronger for the experience. Grey skies, on the other hand, work in a more insidious way, choking off the psyche's basic need for light and leaving the body listless and unproductive. And it can be deadly. Suicide rates spike in the darkest months. Looked at this way, a cheap charter to Cancun can be regarded as a good investment, if not an act of outright self-preservation.

The question is, is this annual migration to the sunbelt all that it's cracked up to be? I was put in mind of this recently when I ran into my old friend Pat, a much more ambitious traveller than I who goes to places like New Zealand and South Africa. He and Laura had just come back from a month in Patagonia. I made the usual envious noises, feeling sorry for myself at not having managed a SAD break for the third year in a row, but he was having none of it. "You're better off here," he steamed. "I'm so sick of living out of a suitcase, getting ripped off every time you turn around and never getting a decent night's sleep. With the money we spend travelling, we could build a home theatre with HDTV. None of these places look as good in real life as they do on OLN anyway. Or we could take an extra two weeks off in the summer and enjoy BC. We have the best scenery in the world, and the food doesn't make you sick. I'm never getting on one of those sardine-can charters again."

Funny how often people just back from long excursions talk this way. Even on our low-budget jaunts, we are always glad to come home to our familiar bed. Leaving aside the obvious hassles of lost luggage, *tourista* that won't quit, sunstroke and relentless rip-off, even the stress-free breaks often seem to leave you wondering, "Are we having fun yet?" I remember standing on top of the Pyramid of the Sun thinking, "Gee, this looks just like it did on OLN TV except only about one-tenth as high." And the Lonely Planet guy somehow managed to visit it on a day when it wasn't crawling with out-of-puff Midwesterners twanging into their digicams. It just never seems to live up to the expectations you had daydreaming about it back in Old Soggy.

Here's the odd thing, though: even if the actual on-the-road experience doesn't rise above the level of a fairly good time, it changes when you look back on it. When I first read Paul Theroux's famous verdict "travel is glamorous only in retrospect," I didn't know what he was talking about. I've since learned. Somehow those travel experiences that were so-so at the time take root in the memory and blossom with passing years into something fully as glorious as you ever daydreamed they would be. All the miseries of daylong waits in godforsaken airports wither away, leaving only the high points. It's something to cling to as you lie awake in a 2-star hacienda sweating and fretting about whether the Mexican car rental is going to have you jailed for caving in the bumper of their new Fit while running back and forth to the seatless john every five minutes. "Someday," you can tell yourself, "I'm going to be back sitting at my desk in Pender Harbour enjoying the hell out of this." Given how doubtful the travel experiences mostly were at the time, it's remarkable how much time I spend wistfully reliving them later as I put away dishes or shuffle papers back here north of 49. And once you realize travel is mainly useful for restocking your memory banks, you can feel a bit more relaxed about missing the odd turn. Still, three in a row is too many.

A Coaster Discovers Scotland

When my niece Kathleen announced she was getting married and not only that, she was going to do it in Scotland, Mary and I surprised everybody by going along. We would have been forgiven for begging off because of the distance, but Kathleen is our favourite niece, and not just because she's the only one in a batch of five boys. She used to be such a shy little violet I cringed at the thought of her ever facing the cold, cruel world on her own. Now here she was a confident, accomplished young beauty with enough moxie to marry a guy from a country where the men talk funny and wear skirts, and we wanted to show our support.

Besides, we had never been to Scotland. Like many Canadian families, ours is top-heavy with Scotch ancestors. Carmichaels, Cummings, Morrisons, McLeods—even old "Portuguese Joe" Silvey was rumoured to be half-Scotch, courtesy of a provisioning stop in the Azores by a sea captain named Simmons. The most direct link in our family was through my maternal grandmother, who grew up on the Isle of Lewis in the Outer Hebrides, and she wasn't my favourite relative. She was grim and formidable and used to pray in Gaelic at the top of her lungs, a very scary spectacle for a young kid. One of her favourite stories was about the time she chased the tax collector off her farm with a naily 2 x 4, and nobody doubted it. When I first heard the term *battleaxe*, I couldn't help but picture Gramma out there on the blasted moor whaling away with her naily 2 x 4. Later on when it came to allocating our few precious vacation days, going to a whole country full of Grammas didn't exert much pull. We'd been to a lot of other places like Italy and France and Cuba with fewer ancestral ties and better weather, but Scotland had never topped the list of places to go for a good time.

But thanks to our adventurous niece, we finally made it, and are glad we did. Scotland isn't formidable at all. It has a well-developed inferiority complex, thanks to its domineering southern neighbour, which makes a Canadian feel right at home. There is something familiar about the way they make much of local athletes who place an honourable fourth at Wimbledon and writers who are shortlisted for the Booker Prize but don't actually win it. There is much grumbling in Edinburgh's countless pubs about the revenue from Scotland's oil fields flowing south and never coming back that also strikes a sympathetic chord in the Canadian breast.

I admit to having felt a bit of Scottish overexposure at times with all our pipe bands, highland flings, caber tossing and haggis-laden Robbie Burns nights, but the good news is that Scots have a reciprocal interest in things Canadian. This is possibly the one foreign country you can go to where Canada is not thought of as a pimple on the US backside. When a Scot asks you where you're from and you say Canada, you might be surprised by the reply, "Aye, a ken tha, but wha province like?" More than once when the conversation drilled down as far as actually mentioning the Sunshine Coast, I was amazed to hear something like, "Aye, a bonnie place. Me brrrother lives in Sechelt and we go therrre often." (They do still talk like that.) Wherever we went, we found the general knowledge of things Canadian excellent, certainly far better than in the US.

The Scotch were great travellers historically and that seems to hold true today, partly because the North Sea petroleum industry has spawned a generation of experts who are in high demand wherever there's oil. That might explain why a favourite Canadian destination seems to be Calgary. At the same time, we had the damnedest time getting Scots to tell us anything useful about their own country. They're intensely proud of it, yes, but in a theoretical way that apparently doesn't require them to move around in it much. We grew accustomed to hearing Glaswegians say, "Off ta Edinburgh are ye? Haven't ben therrre since a' was a wee bairn." (It's just under an hour's drive.)

When we mentioned we planned to take a drive through the Highlands, our host said, "Why?" Inverness, the pretty Highland hub closer to Edinburgh than Kelowna is to Vancouver, might be the dark side of the moon for all the Lowlanders who've gone there. It put me in mind of the Sunshine Coast's own one-way migration pattern where northerners make regular trips south to shop and travel but southerners can grow up and grow old without visiting their neighbours an hour's drive north. Too bad, the homebound Lowlanders miss vast vistas of Elphinstone-sized mountains covered in nothing but a solid pink blanket of heather. Just like the pricey little nursery-bought sprigs that keep dying out in my rockery back home, but thousands of acres of it growing wild, making the whole landscape seem like a vast shrub garden. I don't know how a Scotch mountain decides whether to grow heather or trees, because some are forested (and checkered with BC-style cutblocks) but intermixed with these will be other mountains carpeted with nothing but a lavender frizz of heather. One seems to exclude the other.

And of course, lots of broom everywhere. My first impulse upon driving through miles of the stuff was to think, "They should do something about this before it takes over." Then I remembered: "Oh yeah, there's a reason it's called Scotch broom. It's native here." For a moment I found myself wondering why we have programs to eradicate it back on the Sunshine Coast. If you just accept it like the Scots do, it begins to look kind of nice. Same with thistles. The weed has the run of the place, like cattle in India. When one with a head the size of a small cabbage spiked me near the Highland shrine on Culloden Moor, I forgot for a moment that it is Scotland's sacred national symbol and stomped it flat. From the glares I got, you'd think I'd peed on the Stone of Scone.

After careening around the country on the wrong side of the road for a week I was left to wonder why I'd never realized that Scotland is a carbon copy of BC, at least the Highland part. I guess it was the language barrier. When I read all that Walter Scott and Robbie Burns palaver about bens, firths, glens and lochs, I somehow missed that they were just talking about plain old BC-style mountains, inlets, valleys and lakes. There was a lot of flora along the highway that looked familiar, with only slight differences from our versions when studied up close. There were great hillside patches of something that by any other name was still fireweed. So much for claiming that clearcut colonizer as a unique New World emblem.

It's no wonder Scots pioneers found this country such a good fit and came here in such numbers. Not only were they used to year-round rain, they were expert loggers and fishermen. In fact, when we were there in 2011, their forest industry was still employing forty thousand workers (more than in BC) and their fishing industry was still supplying 60 per cent of Britain's seafood, though I understand there has been some slippage since. Remote communities like Ullapool, Oban, Lerwick and Anstruther were not only postcard-pretty, they had thriving commercial trawl fleets. You couldn't help but marvel at these industries still chugging along after untold centuries when we in BC have basically mismanaged ours to near ruin in a fragment of the time. It was enough to make you wish those old Scots pioneers had brought a little more of their Old World planning smarts with them when they set up over here.

We thought two weeks would be more than enough to do such a small country, but it just whetted our appetite. Thanks to Kathleen and our renewed Scottish ties, we can't wait to go back.

Trading in the Rain

It's a curious fact of life here in BC, which didn't even exist two lifetimes ago, that we are fully as enthralled with our history as parts of the country that have been settled since the 1500s. BC churns out more books fondly remembering old times than Ontario and Quebec combined, and I should know since I am guilty of churning many. But I wouldn't do it if there weren't so many people out there ferociously scribbling down their memories and so many others eagerly lapping them up. I occasionally tried a book about current affairs and I still have most of the copies growing mould in my warehouse. BC folks love casting their minds back. I don't know if that is a comment on the quality of our present lives or not.

There is one curious blind spot in our constant re-examination of our brief and spotty historical record however, that I find passing strange. It's not some minor detail either—it is one of the most in-your-face aspects of daily life. Business. Commerce. Trade. You might think with all the resources business has at its disposal and all the energy it puts into moulding public opinion, it would leave a strong imprint on the historical record, but such is not the case.

Just think of some of the BC companies that dominated public life just a few years back—Woodward's Stores. MacMillan Bloedel. BC Packers. BC Tel. Pacific Western Airlines. Cunningham Drugs.

Bow-Mac. Chan TV. Ubiquitous just a decade (or two?) ago, these names are now vanishing like footprints in wet sand. Given a few more years they will be as untraceable as the once-omnipresent W.H. Malkin, Edward Lipsett, Begg Motors, Spencer's Department Stores, Evans Coleman Evans, and McLennan, McFeely and Prior—companies that dominated the landscape of my youth but are now unknown even to the omniscient bots of Google.

Should we care, you may well ask. Not necessarily, I guess. I just point out that it's weird that these companies that are such a part of our lives simply dry up and blow away leaving hardly a trace. It's easy to see why the companies are that way—they survive only by looking forward and find little profit in preserving their past, which often as not has some bothersome skeletons in it. But why historians don't pay a little more attention, I don't know.

Here on the coast, the same holds true. I think of some of the businesses that shaped the community I knew growing up here. Of course everybody is tired of hearing about the Union Steamships Co. that kept us connected with the outer world before the day of BC Ferries. But what about Tidewater Transport? That was the little one-ship freight line that served the coast when I was a kid, filling in with a converted sub-chaser called the *Jervis Express* after the Union Steamships gave up, but I feel like the only person left alive who remembers that. Likewise, I wonder how many remember Harry Winn, Harry Smith, Hill's Machine Shop, Morgan's Men's Wear, Books and Stuff, *Coast News*, Fred Cruise, John and Fran Burnside, Frank Solnik, Frank White, Tommy Ono, Rose Nicholson, Dale Burns, "Tiny" at Sechelt Agencies, Sid McDonnell, Frank Harding, Clint Anderson, Kay Hatashita, Joe Benner, Helen Bishop, Peter Grabenhof, Lang's Drugs, Vic Franske, Jack and Lee Redmond, Billy May, Hill's Machine Shop, Colonel Flounder, Olli Sladey Realty, Al Campbell's Tyee Airways, Ben Lang's Drugs, Joe Benner's Furniture, Wigard's Shoes, Jack

Nelson Barbershop and Taxi, Drs. Alan and Hugh Inglis ... all household names in their day; gone without a trace today. (I am confident this list will ignite sparks of remembrance in anyone resident on the coast c. 1950–80. My apologies to all other readers—this may be the only chance most of these names will ever have to be in a book.)

In the early days, storekeepers were king. The name "Sunshine Coast," after all, was a promotional gimmick from the hyperactive imagination of Harry Roberts, whose grocery store, motel and sawmill made him the mogul of Roberts Creek before he decided he had overdeveloped the place and set off for quieter surroundings on Nelson Island in 1923. Sechelt's commercial history began—and almost ended—with a young English fireball named Bert Whitaker, who bought up ¾ mile of the Trail Bay waterfront and began a spectacular ascendancy as hotelier, steamboater and logging boss in 1895, and capped it off with a spectacular bankruptcy in 1925. But all was not lost—Whittaker's cousin E.S. Clayton revived family fortunes with a new Sechelt store (hands up all who remember the "Tomboy Store") that over the years morphed into the present Trail Bay Shopping Centre.

Up in Pender Harbour, ex-Madeira islander "Portuguese Joe" Gonsalves married an Indigenous woman from Burrard Inlet and set himself up for a thirty-year run as laird of the community, building a store, hotel and fish dock in 1904. His name is not as fully obliterated as some, surviving on one of the main arteries of Madeira Park, BC—or would be if the highways department hadn't misspelled the road name "Gonzales." Portuguese Joe, Bob Donley, Gil Mervin, Sis Hassan, Al Lloyd—the successive owners of Pender Harbour's general stores were the community's royalty and oldtimers could recite their names like schoolchildren reciting the succession of English kings. When I was a kid the leading light was a man named Royal Murdoch and I thought his name must be a kind of title bestowed upon him by fearful debtors. For aptronyms, though, nobody could top the late-fifties operator of the Irvines Landing store and fuel dock, Milo Filgas.

In my time the title of leading tycoon had long since been surrendered to A.A. Lloyd, who presided over Lloyd's General Store in Garden Bay. Lloyd was an articulate Englishman who used his sharp wit and booming voice to dominate every facet of local life, serving as School Trustee and Chamber of Commerce head and unofficial banker to whom everyone had to kowtow to keep their grocery credit safe. His wife was addressed as "Queenie," a title she accepted, and together they played the role of small-town royalty to the hilt. Respectability wasn't in plentiful supply in Pender in those days, but what there was of it the Lloyds had locked up. So it caused quite a stir when the redoubtable Mr. Lloyd was discovered in the arms of a foxy young fishwife whose husband was away for the salmon season—and who was, to sound a much-needed point of continuity here, the daughter of the aforementioned Harry Roberts.

Lloyd did the right thing and sent Queenie packing and installed his new missus in the house on the hill, but this young woman had a mind of her own. She persuaded Lloyd to buy a sailboat, moved the family aboard and began flirting with the tune-in, turn-on, drop-out element that was invading the coast at that time. Lloyd gamely tried to keep up, even to the point of joining skinny-dipping parties up at Bear Lake, or "Bare-Ass Lake" as local wags began spelling it. I remember an oldtimer named Sam Hately shaking his head after driving past a middle-aged man strolling along Irvines Landing Road in the altogether and just about steering into the lake when he realized it was none other than that former bastion of respectability, A.A. Lloyd. "I dunno, this just isn't the world I recognize anymore," he mused.

In time the world returned to a more recognizable shape and so did A.A Lloyd, who got his clothes back on, gave his wife the keys to the sailboat, built a new house on another hill and spent a long retirement MC'ing May Days and being thoroughly boring.

It's wonderful what you can find if you scratch just a little beneath the dull exterior of small-town life.

Down at the south end of the Sunshine Coast, the main business from the 1920s until the 1950s was Howe Sound Trading Company, operated out of Gibsons by J.H. Drummond, who delivered orders of groceries, gumboots, horseshoe nails and Dr. Browne's Chlorodyne (containing alcohol, opium, cannabis and chloroform) as far up coast as Wilson Creek in his Model T Ford.

As commerce matured, the coast began to attract more diversified businesses than general stores and hotels. Wilf Scott evolved his informal delivery service into Wilf Scott Transfer, the area's first franchised freight service. Pear-shaped, cigar-chewing Cec Lawrence bought the old jitney service and grew it into a respectable bus line called Sechelt Motor Transport, anchored by a resplendent red-brick bus station at Wharf Road and Cowrie Street. Morgan Thompson, a shy man whose only topic of conversation was the state of Sechelt's retail economy, operated Morgan's Men's Wear (later Georgian Traders) for his entire life, it seemed. Norm Watson and Bernel Gordon were two Sechelt entrepreneurs I remember mainly for their erudition. Watson ran Tyee Products which sold sport fishing bait under the slogan BEST PROCURABLE PONDED HERRING. Snappy. I'm not sure what Bernel's game was, possibly insurance, but he seemed to spend most of his time ambling up and down the Cowrie Street sidewalk jawing with everyone he met. His greeting was never anything as simple as "Hi there"; it would be something along the lines of "Felicitations, my good sir! To quote Macbeth, 'So fair and foul a day I have not seen.'" He and Watson were both perennial aldermen and their verbal jousting would prolong council meetings late into the night, filling whole pages of the next week's papers. You just don't hear many seven-syllable words in today's sound-bite politics, and I sort of miss it.

As the highways improved and the automobile count rose, gas stations proliferated. Oil companies in the fifties and sixties seemed to adhere to the dictum "the more the merrier," just as today they seem to feel none is too many. Today I count eight on the entire coast, whereas when my dad had Pender Harbour Chevron there were eight in Pender Harbour alone and over thirty on the whole coast. Most of the operators weren't chamber of commerce types and a lot of them—Reg Jackson, Frank Solnik, Tommy Ono, Bill Copping and Cliff Connor—were the kind of characters you don't find in today's convenience-store operations. They weren't so quick to wipe your windshield maybe, and would probably leave it dirtier if they tried, but they could overhaul your engine while delivering a bone-shaking rant on everything that was wrong with the modern world. One of the more memorable was a guy named Cunningham who had a B/A station halfway up Halfmoon Bay Hill. This Cunningham was six-foot-ten and his wife was about six-four. They had met at the Tip Toppers Club. They were a sight to behold. Either one of them had to bend over just about double to ask you if you wanted a fill-up.

Halfmoon Bay was a much remoter location then than it is today, and to make things worse, there was a competing Shell station at the bottom of the hill. What kept Cunningham in business was Cunningham's Corner. This was before Halfmoon Hill had been straightened and widened and just after it passed their gas station it lurched down a very steep pitch, followed by a deceptive, improperly banked curve. On Saturday nights it was just like the demolition derby out there, and Cunningham's tow truck would be going steady pulling wrecks out of the rockpile beside the hairpin.

A lot of the victims were a bit worse for wear and this gave the Cunninghams the idea of supplementing their tow truck business with an ambulance, of which there were none in the area at that time. They weren't that well capitalized, and the ambulance they got was one of those old stretch Cadillacs like Bill Murray drove in *Ghostbusters*. Mostly those supersized Caddies were used as hearses, and I'm not sure but this one had been a hearse in its previous life. Anyway, Mrs. Cunningham took a first-aid course and they were in business as the coast's first ambulance service. Right away, they were run off their size-eighteen feet.

The problem was, Mr. C had a problem. The same problem that a lot of his ambulance customers had: he liked to sit down after a hard day's work and relax with a drink or three. Catch him late in the evening and the chances were he'd be listing to port a little. When you are six-foot-ten, it is not easy to hide a slight list. It's much harder to stay balanced up on those stilts of legs, and any tendency to reel and wallop about is much more exaggerated than it is in someone built closer to the ground. After a half-dozen beers he looked like John Cleese doing the Funny Walk. Add to this, Mr. C was not a happy tippler. The more he imbibed the more his bedside manner deteriorated. These two factors may have combined to make Mr. C's performance on the rescue circuit seem more alarming than it really was, I don't know, but soon there were stories of badly injured motorists begging to be left on the roadside rather than chance it in the Cunninghams' Ectomobile. It was a ticklish situation, because an ambulance service was sorely needed, and the Cunninghams were in denial about the problem.

It wasn't long after that government ambulances began showing up on the coast, and who knows, maybe the Cs' interesting problem accelerated the arrival of that excellent service. In time the Cunninghams gave up and moved off coast, grumbling about unfair competition.

Somehow our businesses today seem so bland by comparison.

A Swan among the Seagulls

Some doctors achieve the status of folk heroes in the communities they serve and this is about one such man, although you will have to take my word for it because it is not something the late Dr. Alan Swan would ever have dreamed of claiming for himself and he certainly doesn't do so in his excellent memoir, *House Calls by Float Plane*.

I can remember when Dr. Swan first showed up in the old Anglican mission hospital in Pender Harbour and how welcome a sight he was. I was just a nine-year-old kid at the time but I had plenty of reason to be glad at the prospect of an upgrade in local medical services. Pender Harbour's little wood-frame hospital was not a favoured setting for medical careers, and since its founding in 1930 by the Anglican Church–run Columbia Coast Mission it had suffered from a revolving door, doctor-wise. Often there was no doctor on staff at all and when there was, it was someone who was only there because he wouldn't be allowed to practise in any place that had a choice.

This had been the case two years before when I tripped running down the gangplank at Murdoch's General Store and broke both bones in my left arm clean off an inch above the wrist. I was rushed over to the hospital and attended upon by an ill-tempered old sawbones named Dr. Tripp, who slapped on a plaster cast without bothering to set the bones straight, so that when the cast

49

came off my left hand was offset like a box-end spanner. Dr. Tripp claimed to see nothing wrong, so my parents went to the trouble of making a special trip to a pediatrician in faraway Vancouver, who was so appalled at Tripp's hack job that he considered re-breaking the bones but in the end decided to take a chance the arm would straighten as I grew—which it fortunately did.

The hard-pressed superintendent of the mission, the Rev. Alan Greene (he would be Canon-ized later), supported the cost of running the hospital by going around to boss loggers like my father with his hand out, and next time he chugged into our camp in his bible boat the *John Antle IV*, my father told him what he thought of Dr. Tripp, but it didn't matter—even that incompetent had found Pender Harbour unworthy to his aspirations and had since decamped, leaving the Sechelt Peninsula doctorless once again.

It was into this dire situation Dr. Swan wandered in 1954, intending to spend a couple years assisting his former medical school classmate John Playfair and getting some experience while he and his new bride Rosa shopped around for a more worthwhile place to set down roots in. Playfair had similar intentions and upped stakes after a short period, but Swan fell in love with the rustic little fishing and logging community and, except for a four-year stint as an itinerant doctor to First Nations in northern British Columbia, spent the rest of his working life in the area.

We couldn't believe our luck. Dr. Swan was a fine specimen of a man, both mentally and physically. He was a great strapping fellow who looked like he would be at home playing professional football, but his manner was as compassionate and gentle as his physique was imposing. Blessed with a photographic memory that became the stuff of legend, he never forgot a name, or any one of Pender Harbour's Byzantine family relationships. He was a recent graduate of Queen's University in Kingston and up on the latest medical knowledge. He had seemingly endless stamina to go with his good heart and expert technique, and worked round the clock, never hesitating to make house calls to the most landlocked homestead or camp. Better, he attracted other young, competent doctors like Eric Paetkau and Walter Burtnick to the area and gave leadership to a group who eventually ushered the Sunshine Coast into the modern era of health care.

Today the region Dr. Swan ventured into in 1954 is home to some thirty thousand residents served by some twenty-five doctors spread out between the centres of Gibsons, Sechelt and Pender Harbour. There is a modern sixty-three-bed hospital centrally located in Sechelt and a well-equipped community health centre in Pender Harbour. In 1954, the area population was approximately seventy-five hundred and the only medical facility was the thirteen-bed mission hospital, which was awkwardly located at the north end of the territory in Pender Harbour. This lopsided arrangement had made more sense when the mission started its medical service in 1930 because that was the era of marine transport when the bays and islands of Jervis and Sechelt Inlets were swarming with small gyppo logging camps and Pender Harbour with its fine all-weather shelter offered the most logical spot for all these far-flung outposts to congregate in their small workboats. As time went on however, road travel outpaced the marine variety and population growth at the south end of the Sunshine Coast far outstripped that in the north, where the myriad logging camps up Jervis Inlet closed for lack of timber. This process would have just begun when Dr. Swan appeared on the coast and was well advanced by the time he had been practising for five years.

The result was that most of the work that was to be done was separated from the wonky little hospital where it had to be performed by the length of the Sunshine Coast highway, which in those days was no highway at all, but a series of interconnected logging roads whose up-and-down dimension in the form of world-record chuckholes, Swan speculates in his book, almost matched its lateral dimension. This was especially problematic for expectant mothers, who were forced to undertake the epic, jarring journey at a time they could least endure it. More than a few new coasters ended up being shaken into the world along the way. Nevertheless, Swan and his partners birthed some one thousand babies at the old St. Mary's during his ten years there, personally accounting for a whole generation of Sunshine Coast population increase. No wonder there are so many middle-aged men named "Al" in the Sunshine Coast phone book today!

History vs. Hotdogs

Given our penchant for celebrating anniversaries that might better be forgotten, like the Vancouver Canucks' fifty years of futility in pursuit of the Stanley Cup, it is surprising that more wasn't made a few years ago of the diamond jubilee of the coastal ferry service.

Or maybe not.

The ferry corp is not exactly a popular topic these days. Sailings have never been more unpredictable, the fares have never been higher, the ridership has plateaued—and its senior executives can't stop counting up their giant bonus cheques long enough to connect up the dots between those things.

But despite its current funk it's hard to think of one thing that transformed life on this coast as profoundly as the arrival of the car ferry and it doesn't reflect well on our self-awareness that the sixtieth anniversary passed almost without comment. I wouldn't have known myself but for a web posting by online historian Gary Little, and that's bad because I must be one of the few living coastians who actually partook in the event.

It's one of my first memories of life on the Sunshine Coast after my family moved to Nelson Island. I would have been six on August 11, 1951, and details are a little dim, but I recall the long, punishing ride down the rutted logging road that passed for a highway in those days in the rattletrap six-door jitney that passed for a bus. My dad didn't own a car. There probably weren't two dozen operational motor vehicles on the Sunshine Coast in those days, if you don't count the ones used for hauling logs. There wasn't much use for private vehicles because the few roads that existed were such that you risked taking out a crankcase or differential every fifty yards. At several points during our transit from Pender Harbour to Gibsons, the able-bodied male passengers were called upon to get out and push the jitney up washboardy hills and there were several level creek-crossings where the driver had to hit the water at top speed and kind of drift across. But mainly as a result of the event we were off to witness on that day, traffic would be streaming up a new highway to Powell River within three years and the automobile age would be transforming life throughout the Sunshine Coast.

Dad had enticed me along for the ride by saying there was going to be a big celebration in Gibsons to mark the start-up of ferry service, including a boxing match, which excited me. Not that I cared about boxing, but I reckoned an outing like that would be sure to include popcorn and hotdogs and other fun things seldom encountered on Nelson Island. When we got to Gibsons however, Dad presented me with a choice: we could stay there and take in the festivities around town or we could actually embark on the ferry on its first trip.

"It's a chance to be a part of history," he told me.

I didn't know what history was exactly, but the way Dad spoke of it, it sounded at least as exciting as boxing. Alas, the crossing on the antique *Quillayute* offered no more to relieve boredom than its modern counterpart and I remember thinking I'd been duped.

The new service was operated by the Black Ball Line, a private concern that specialized in starting new crossings—in 1817 it had initiated the first scheduled passenger service across the Atlantic Ocean. Black Ball was headed by an American emissary of free enterprise named, somewhat hilariously it seemed to my six-year-old mind, Captain Peabody. Peabody had been blackballed from operating ferries in Puget Sound after trying to ram through a 30 per cent fare hike, which led Washingtonians to conclude the profit motive didn't serve the needs of a coastal population dependent on marine links. They nationalized Peabody's operation in 1951, replacing it with the Washington State Ferries system, which has provided reliable and affordable service there ever since.

Peabody managed to hang on to several old boats Washington didn't want and shifted to BC waters, where he hoped to build a new ferry empire free of state interference. At first it seemed a good move for him and BC both, but the BC government soon came to the same conclusion as its Washington counterpart and in 1961 the redoubtable captain found himself nationalized a second time when BC premier W.A.C. Bennett merged Black Ball into the BC Ferry Authority. The rest, as my father would have said, is history. Peabody's ragtag fleet expanded to fulfill Bennett's vision of a reliable and affordable marine highway that enabled BC's coastal economy to flourish, faltering only when lesser leaders forgot the lessons of the past and began confusing the mandates of public utilities with those of private industry.

Until I read Gary Little's article I thought the sailing my dad and I took that August day in 1951 was merely the BC ferry system's first crossing of Howe Sound. I assumed the Vancouver Island run had started earlier. Now, thanks to Gary's website, I realize that the Island crossings had not yet begun and that trip on the shimmying, shuddering old *Quillayute* was the Black Ball-cum-BC Ferries' first official trip in BC ever. It was more historic even than my father claimed. Not that I would have cared at the time. I just wanted a hotdog.

Sex on the Sunshine Coast

To my knowledge, sex on the Sunshine Coast began in 1955. Before that there wasn't any. At least to my knowledge. I base this on personal observation. I had spent my entire conscious life on the Sunshine Coast and can't remember ever even encountering the word *sex* up until that time. Life seemed to go along fine without it. I lived in a logging camp on Nelson Island an hour away from Pender Harbour by slow boat (fifteen minutes at today's speeds) where my dad and his crew of mostly off-season Pender Harbour fishermen, who he referred to unflatteringly as "gumboot loggers," wrestled trees off the hillside and into the saltchuck. I was a close and fascinated observer of their struggles with old war-surplus logging trucks, haywire yarders that had once been run by steam but now had gas motors bolted across the old boiler frames, Easthope boat motors that always seemed to have water in the gas or else wet Ford ignition coils, and so on. It was a busy place with all sorts of personal dramas—like the time Harry Reiter the boom man sunk an axe into his calf and my mum had to bandage it up and the time my dog Mickey got distemper and had to be shot. But this was all done without sex.

Some puzzling things went on, but they were explainable. For instance, my mother had a secret drawerful of balloons. They were odd little balloons, long and tubular and rather drab in appearance. We kids thought she must have been saving them as a surprise for one of our birthdays, because when she caught me and my sisters playing with them she sort of went nuts, which was quite unusual for that normally unflappable woman. She claimed they weren't for birthdays at all but "for sick people." My mum wasn't a big fan of sex, as I would come to know later after sex became known. There must have been a lot of sick people on the Sunshine Coast in those days because one of the most common items us kids found when we were out in our rowboat beachcombing for items to stock in our pretend general store were more of these sick balloons, usually broken and tattered and often reduced to just a circular rim, which nevertheless made a nifty bracelet for a seven-year-old wrist. One particularly lucky day I found about a dozen of them, six for each wrist, which I proudly displayed to the boys in the big bunkhouse. It had a surprising effect. I was always trying to impress those boys and seldom succeeding, but this time I hit the jackpot. They were literally laughing themselves purple.

"Did you see what the kid's got on his wrists?"

"Holy moly Howie, where did you get those things?"

"Are those trophies from all your conquests, Howie?"

"You better not let your old man see what you've been up to!"

"No, you should show him. He'll be proud of ya!"

I did show him, and he was not proud. I think he even swore, and told me to take them off and flush them down the toilet. I did as told, which meant the mysterious rubber bracelets would be floating ashore again the next day, since all the toilets in camp had straight pipes into the bay.

A lot of stuff went on on the Sunshine Coast I didn't quite understand in those days, including how babies were made. That was until my dad explained it one day when he and I were running the camp boat back to camp around the time my baby brother was born. I could see that babies grew in their mothers' tummies sometimes, but there was no mystery to that. The mums just seemed to make it happen whenever the spirit moved them, like when they decided to start a crock of homebrew. Lil Poschner, the donkey puncher's wife, was always making homebrew and she made babies one after the other, which caused me to wonder if the two hobbies were somehow connected.

I saw no reason to suspect dads had any role in baby-making until this time in the boat when my dad, his tongue loosened after spending most of the day in Gordie Lyons' beer parlour, assured me he had helped make my little brother. The way he drunkenly explained it, when a mum and a dad decided to make a baby they kind of squeezed together and something like a spark jumped from the dad to the mum, which got the baby started.

My dad had grown up in the Bible Belt under the lash of grim Presbyterians and he went all kind of stammery and red-faced when it came to talk of men and women squishing together, like he was in pain or something, which was quite an alarming change to his tough boss-logger demeanour, so I didn't pursue any of the many questions his revelation caused to flare up in my eight-year-old brain. Still, this baby-making procedure sounded more like how a Ford coil worked to start an Easthope boat motor, if it wasn't too wet. It had nothing to do with sex.

When I was ten and my dad and the boys in the big bunkhouse had logged all the available trees on Nelson Island, we closed the Green Bay camp and moved to Pender Harbour, and that was when sex started on the Sunshine Coast. I remember it clearly.

It must have been a weekend because there was no school and I was out playing with the Hatcook kids. There were the twins, Bo and Randy, who were younger and bad, and Sandra, who was my age and nice. We had built a good ten-minute fort out of driftwood in Savolainen's meadow and out of nowhere Randy said, "Well, Bo and me'll take off for a while so you and Sandra can have sex." He had a shorter word for "have sex" but out of respect for my Presbyterian ancestors I will avoid repeating it. In any case, its meaning was just as lost on me as "sex" would have been.

"Okay," I said. "What's sex?"

I knew it was something special because Sandra was yelling and pounding the heck out of Randy, although she seemed to be play-acting mad rather than real mad and both Randy and Bo were laughing their heads off.

"C'mon, tell me," I said. "What's sex?"

"It's what mums and dads do to make babies," Sandra said.

"Oh that," I said. "I know about that."

"Yeah? What do you know?" Randy said. So I told him about the Ford coil process whereby two people squished together and the spark happened.

"You mean they don't even take their clothes off?"

"Why would they do that?"

Once again I found myself on the outside of a group laughing themselves purple for no apparent reason. Eventually I prevailed upon Randy to give his version of how babies were made, which he did with brutal directness. I must say, it struck me as ridiculous, and not a little disgusting. Thanks to my Presbyterian heritage I regarded the body parts reputed to be involved as unfortunate blemishes in God's design, more akin to sewage than babies and love.

Sandra, bless her, shooed her brothers away, sat me down in the driftwood fort, and undertook to convince me otherwise. She did a fair job of it, for which I am grateful to this day.

Anyway, that is how sex came to the Sunshine Coast. After that it started popping up everywhere and has only increased with passing years. At least to my knowledge.

Hollywood Comes to Bute Inlet

One of the odder revelations to drift down from the upper coast in recent years is that a private luxury resort has been built at Leask Cove in Bute Inlet, reputedly for the aging Hollywood bombshell Michelle Pfeiffer. A more unlikely party spot would be hard to imagine, though its getaway value is good.

Of all the BC coast's mainland inlets, none is more forbidding than Bute. Its shores are sheer and offer almost no shelter from the cruel winds that rumble like a coal train down its eighty-kilometre length much of the year. It tends to be dark because of its high sides and the waters are frigid owing to the glacial runoff from the massive icefields draping Mount Waddington at its head. It was once a centre of attention when a group of Victoria entrepreneurs proposed it as a route for the first cross-Canada railroad, but its formidable terrain and vile weather defeated their work crews and precipitated the Chilcotin Uprising, the nearest thing to an "Indian War" in BC history. Ever since, the place has seemed to labour under a curse. Even the Homalco First Nation was eventually forced to abandon its traditional village at Church House near the inlet mouth and move to a subdivision in Campbell River some years back.

One of the few places in the whole inlet to offer a bit of shelter is the little bay below Fawn Bluff known as Leask Cove, and this is where Ms. Pfeiffer apparently sought refuge from the outside world, some fifty kilometres beyond the end of the last road connecting to civilization.

The Leask boys must have been spinning in their graves at the news. They were among the few settlers to make a stand in Bute Inlet, and Leask Cove was the site of their homestead. Leask Lake, which feeds a small creek into the bay, is also named for them. I wish I knew more about them. The little I do know I learned from the late Canon Alan Greene, the seagoing missionary who worked the Vancouver–Kingcome Inlet beat for the Anglican Church from 1911 to 1959, managed the original St. Mary's Hospital in Pender Harbour, gave his name to Sechelt's Greenecourt Seniors Housing centre and spent his retirement years just down the road from me in Halfmoon Bay. The coast was littered with characters of the most memorable type in Canon Greene's heyday and he knew most of them, but the Leask brothers were among his favourites. They were three retired Scottish bachelors who for some unknown reason chose to come to Canada and build their dream estate in that little notch on Bute's inhospitable shore now named in their memory. Maybe it was the closest thing they could find to the storm-blasted Orkney Islands of home. According to their family they arrived in 1913 and held out until 1934.

The Leask brothers were all professional men and evidently about as eccentric as you could get. One was named Charles, another Alfred and the third Henry. They made a good team because each had a specialty that complemented the other. One had been a banker, one an accountant and the other a New Zealand sea captain who joined the team a few years into their Bute experiment, after growing blindness disqualified him from piloting ships. The three of them laboured day and night to terrace their stony hillside and fit it out with every technological improvement. Their home was full of well-thumbed books on every topic from electrical engineering to Shakespeare, and they were always eager to receive any new reading material from passersby, even months-old newspapers. They fed the little creek into a water-wheel that powered their small sawmill and made theirs one of the few electrified homesteads on the coast. They had an abundant garden, an orchard and a herd of goats to provide milk and cheese. Vegetables were stored in a commodious stone root cellar built into the sidehill. They occupied themselves studying and arguing about philosophy and pursuing sophisticated hobbies.

"When you came there, one would say, 'Oh, you must come and have a look at Henry's water-wheel!'" Canon Greene recalled. "They had a very complex small-scale hydroelectric system that provided them with electricity.

"While the one brother demonstrated its wonders, the one who made it would stand to the side saying, 'Really, Alan, it's only a Pelton wheel and a crude one at that.'"

"Then they would take you to see Alfred's garden, showing off the rare herbs and foot-long beans while Alfred stood aside saying, 'I should have had six more rows of those if I was doing my job.'"

Charles was an enthusiastic painter who did his best with the local landscape in a style that owed less to Gainsborough than to Grandma Moses, and would stand to one side while his brothers showed his latest creations muttering, "The composition is rather off on that one" and "I didn't get Mount Elphinstone quite right, I'm afraid."

"One brother fell and broke a leg while working in the garden," said Greene. "The other two set the bones in a cast of their own design. They also constructed a special chair, a fantastic-looking thing with a long, protruding rest for the injured leg and handles along the side so they could carry him about. After a few weeks they decided to take him to our mission hospital at Rock Bay in their little gasboat and I remember seeing the three of them coming up the path with this fantastic chair, the two healthy brothers walking on each side and the injured one seated rather like a small-time rajah except for the protruding leg."

The doctor looked at the leg and told them there was nothing he could do. They had done as well as anyone could and the bone was firmly set.

One spring Greene rolled in to find one of the brothers had spent the winter industriously creating a large telescope. It was a wonder of precision, and the old gent had personally melted the glass for the lenses and ground them by hand. It was set up on the veranda overlooking the inlet and they wouldn't let Greene sit down until he had tested it. He found it to be a marvel of clarity and enlargement. The only trouble was, there was nothing to see across the empty expanse of Bute Inlet. As Greene told me, "I put my eye to the thing and all I could see was trees on the far shore. I removed my eye and all I could see was the same trees, except not quite so tall. It seemed a lot of trouble to go to to make those infernal trees half an inch taller."

Another time they came rushing down to meet him all excited about their new diet. They claimed to have made a study of human physiology and devised the perfect sustenance. No sooner was Greene in the door than they plopped a bowl in front of him. It contained a substance that looked and tasted like papier mâché, but with faint traces of kerosene. He begged off after a mouthful, saying delectable as it was, he had just eaten.

Despite the wondrous diet (or perhaps because of it), Charles eventually fell ill and died. Without him, the labour of maintaining their foothold on the inhospitable shore of Bute Inlet fell upon the increasingly decrepit backs of Alfred and Henry, and they nearly starved. Then Bute's weather struck a particularly violent blow in 1934, with the result both surviving brothers were injured trying to protect their property. Locals came to their rescue and removed them to hospital. For years that was where the story ended for me and I was left to assume they quietly faded away in some Lower Mainland care facility. Canon Greene died in 1972 and I never expected to come across any fresh intelligence about this cobwebby little corner of coastal history that I sometimes wondered if anyone else on earth was aware of, much less cared about. I hoped someday I might stumble across a faded clipping in an archive that would confirm Canon Greene's stories and give me a bit more to go on. I never dreamed the internet would have anything to do with it.

Then one day while googling Bute Inlet in an unrelated quest, up popped an image titled "Fawn Bluff" bearing the signature of one C. Leask that could only be a painting of the brothers' homestead at its zenith. The sturdy house, the sawmill, the garden, orchard, henhouse, toolshed, penstock and power house were all there in meticulous detail. The only thing missing was any sign of the three occupants themselves. However, the foreground was enlivened by a conspicuous floating log bearing three disputatious seagulls, screeching at each other and jockeying for position. A private joke sifting down through the years, perhaps?

This apparent visual confirmation gave me the confidence to re-post the image on the KnowBC.com Blog together with the sketchy bits of Leask information I could recall, and lo and behold, comments began trickling in from far-flung corners of the globe confirming not only lost details of the brothers' existence, but that they still had living relatives.

Pauline spoke up from New Zealand in 2014 to say:
hi im a Leask and they sound alot like the strong Orkney people we decend from and came to central otago New Zealand.

Graeme weighed in from Dublin, Ireland, in 2015 to add:
The brothers Leask were my great grandfather's first cousins. Charles died first and Alfred and Henry nearly starved, then were injured in a storm and had to be rescued in 1934. Their nephew Alex Sutherland Leask came from UK to bring them home to Scotland. Henry died a few months later but Alfred recovered.

In 2017 my blog post somehow came to the notice of May Crossling in Edinburgh, who wrote:
These are my relatives, I have a post bag they sent an otter skin back to Edinburgh in which has been kept all these years. My mother has

told me that they went to New Zealand as sheep farmers (my cousin who lives there has identified the land from paintings). They were not successful partly due to sheep rustling. The family said they should return to the UK. They decided to come back via Canada since they had gone out via South Africa, and somehow came to a stop at Fawn Bluff. Alfred spent his final years with my mother's aunts at Newhaven Road in Edinburgh.

Can I just burble for a moment about how amazing I find this? I don't know if I'm more gobsmacked by the knowledge that the Leask legend is based on reality and lives on in both hemispheres, or that the KnowBC Blog has readers—worldwide ones at that. I always assumed that when I posted my thoughts there I was basically talking to myself. No castaway who ever launched a message in a bottle was more surprised to get a reply.

The last time I anchored in Leask Cove, just before its discovery by Hollywood, I spent some time exploring the densely overgrown shelf of land below the towering hillside, but all I could find was an impressive amount of crumbling rockwork, obviously the labour of years. It was always my intention to go back with a machete and see what other clues I could wrestle from the underbrush, but Ms. Pfeiffer's excavators have completed the job of eradicating all trace of the Leask boys' wilderness wonders. Fortunately someone had the good grace to put their name on the cove and lake, so that much will remain at least.

P.S.: The latest report from Fawn Bluff brings the unsurprising news that Ms. Pfeiffer has already found the isolation and storms of Bute Inlet a bit much. This "Quintessential Canadian retreat" is now back on the market for a paltry $28.8 million.

Good Wood

The Cabin is our clan clubhouse, a plywood shack on leased land over at Canoe Pass. By itself the cabin is no architectural wonder, but the wide sundeck that runs along its seaward side is another matter. It's made of seasoned, silvered, fine-grained, clear, fir 2 x 12s. We were over the other day enjoying the gorgeous sunset over Texada and the visitor we had with us couldn't stop staring at these boards. "Where did they *come* from?" he marvelled. "You just don't *see* planks like that anymore."

As with a lotta stuff around here, therein hangs a tale. Those 2 x 12s were custom-milled in the early twentieth century to build one of the early hangars at the original Vancouver airport, but that's not where we got them. They had already been recycled once, into the old Beaver Lumber building on Kingsway.

How did they end up at Canoe Pass? Well, one day back in the seventies I made the mistake of saying to my father that my new hippie chum and I were thinking of starting a newspaper, and would it be okay if I cut some poles on the back lot and put up a poly lean-to for an office? The existing newspaper, the *Peninsula Times*, was making fun of long hair and we wanted to answer back. My father said sure, that sounded like a great idea, but didn't a good newspaper need something a little solider than a plastic lean-to?

Not ours, I said, but even long before he went deaf, Dad had a knack of not hearing certain things.

The next thing I knew he had made a $1,500 deposit on this Beaver Lumber building in Burnaby, which he would lose if the building wasn't torn down and removed from the property in two weeks. It was only a medium-sized building supply, but in the circumstances it seemed the biggest building I'd ever seen. There was nothing I could do but help take the thing down and move it to Pender Harbour so we could build our office so we could publish our newspaper so we could get back at the redneck editor of the *Peninsula Times*. My father had this way of complicating things.

It was November and the weather was vile. My hippie publishing partner lasted until the third day. "I just wanted to write a letter to the editor," he whimpered, sloping off into the blizzard. It was two weeks of hell, but we ended up with enough used building material to rebuild the downtown core of Madeira Park. We built a sturdy 40 x 40 office/print shop for my paper and there was enough left over to build a sturdy 40 x 40 workshop for my father with revenue space overhead. Both were framed out of strong, straight 2 x 12s the like of which you never see today. Some places they were spiked together six-up to make 12 x 12s. Still, this didn't use up all these beautiful, long, straight heritage Douglas fir planks that must have been logged around the time of the First World War and had become so hard over decades of seasoning they rang like iron and made six-inch spikes double over like shingle nails. Some of them were thirty-six feet long, straight, without a knot. It made you feel proud of Canada just to look at them. In fact, Dad was so enthralled by them he wouldn't let us use them all. The very best ones he pulled aside and stacked. "Don't need wood like that for floor joists. Save 'em for the roof." But when it came to the roof, he high-graded the stack again. "Shame to use wood like that if you don't need to."

That was how we ended up with two good buildings and a head-high stack of clear thirty-six-foot 2 x 12s. Specialty wood people used to drive up from the city just on rumour and offer my dad top dollar for that stack, but he just got a faraway look in his eye and thanked them politely for their interest. I used to wake up to the screeching noise of him and Mum out there crowbarring spikes out of them. They restacked them neatly with 1 x 4 spacers between the layers. I used to drop by summer evenings and Mum would be out there in the fading light with a mallet tapping the spacers along so they didn't cause rot. Then she'd get up on top with a broom and sweep off the maple leaves so the moisture wouldn't collect.

Years went by. Mum died. Nobody remembered to pound the spacers along, or sweep the leaves. The planks began to lose their iron-hard ringing noise. When you whacked them with a crowbar it made sort of a thud. That's when our brother-in-law Chas marched up there with his little city-guy chainsaw and started pulling the pile apart and sawing the 2 x 12s into handy lengths to fit in his little city-guy pickup truck. "Better than letting them rot down to nothing," he chirped. The rest of the clan stood by paralyzed and speechless at the sacrilege. But Chas was a city guy and a science teacher and right, and he didn't give a fig for our hillbilly superstitions. He took the best of those memorial 2 x 12s over to the Pass and nailed them down around The Cabin to form that wonderful sundeck where most of our important clan events have since taken place.

You can guess the rest. The remainder of the pile melted down into a heap, and finally somebody bucked up the few remaining solid bits for firewood. Chas died. Dad died. The deck at The Cabin is all that remains. For the sake of our visitor we tried to remember what year it was Chas built that deck, but thinking about it we all got too choked up to talk.

The Princess

Jervis Inlet, which zigzags deep into the Coast Range like a sixty-five-kilometre lightning bolt between the Sechelt Peninsula and the Powell River side, is a classic coastal fjord, shadowed most of its length by mile-high mountain walls. It is very deep and includes a three-thousand-foot hole known as the Jervis Deep, the deepest point anywhere in the Inside Passage. However, the feature that sets Jervis Inlet apart from its sister inlets occurs sixteen kilometres from the head on the east side. There the mountain walls unexpectedly part and let into a six-kilometre side inlet—Princess Louisa—surrounded by such precipitous bluffs the effect is like looking up at the sky from the bottom of a colossal and extremely gorgeous cavern.

"There is no use describing that inlet," author Erle Stanley Gardner once wrote, before proceeding to ignore his own advice:

There is a calm tranquility which stretches from the smooth surface of the reflecting waters straight up into infinity. The deep calm of eternal silence is only disturbed by the muffled roar of throbbing waterfalls as they plunge down from sheer cliffs. There is no scenery in the world that can beat it. Not that I've seen the rest of the world. I don't need to. I've seen Princess Louisa Inlet.

I won't fall into the trap of trying to describe Princess Louisa except to say few Sunshine Coasters would deny it is the Hope

Diamond of the area's scenic jewels. It is the place we take those special visitors we want to hook on the coast, the one experience guaranteed to jar the most jaded soul into a full-blown state of awe. I have been visiting Princess Louisa regularly since I was a kid and it never seems enough. Despite going in many different weathers, moods and ages, it has never failed to send me away with a renewed sense of life's promise.

The inlet's rare magnetism draws remarkable people and inspires them to extraordinary exertions. Legend has it that it was avoided by the Sechelt people after a small village at the head was buried by one of the inlet's periodic rock slides, but band elder Clarence Joe told me his people used to visit it for recreational purposes just as the white man would later.

Early on Princess Louisa was ignored by the more development-minded settlers because its only substantial resource was beauty, which didn't readily lend itself to being canned or milled. This was a challenge inventor Thomas Hamilton would apply himself to later.

Herman Casper just wanted to wake up in the morning and see it. Casper was a deserter from the German army who home-steaded the only decently flat land in the area, the peninsula down at the inlet mouth by Malibu Rapids, in 1900. When he wasn't blacksmithing for local handloggers, Casper whiled away his days spoiling his twenty-six cats and composing songs in praise of the magnificent surroundings, which he was happy to perform with his zither for visiting boaters:

> *Beyond Mount Alfred, in ze vest*
> *Where ze sun goes down to rest*
> *It draws me dere, I don' know vy*
> *S'pose it is ze colour in ze sky.*
> *For zey are purple, mauve and pink*
> *Howeber it makes me vunder, look, and t'ink.*

Casper was followed by Charles "Daddy" Johnstone, a towering mountain man from Daniel Boone country who kept edging west ahead of civilization until he and his six family landed up at Princess Louisa around 1909. There they threw together a one-room split-cedar shack, lived off the land and had three more kids. The Johnstone gang may have succeeded in getting closer to the inlet's soul than anyone since the Sechelt in the days when they had it to themselves. As part of their education, the old man used to send sons Steve and Judd up on the snowy plateau above Princess Louisa without jacket or shoes and only matches, salt and a jackknife for survival. They would live by their wits for weeks at a time, and explore miles into the interior of the province. After World War I, Daddy began to feel that even Jervis was too cramped and carried on to Alaska, where he became a legendary local character all over again. But Steve and Judd returned and passed the rest of their days in homage to the fabulous Jervis landscape that had been so deeply imprinted on them in their formative years. Their names became synonymous with the inlet's wild spirit and Judd in particular became famous for his tall tales of pioneer times.

Judd married Dora Jeffries from Egmont and stayed up Princess Louisa through the birth of their first three girls, a hundred kilometres from the nearest family. The sun would disappear behind the inlet crags for two months in the depths of winter and it would get so cold the salt water would freeze from shore to shore. To get anything that couldn't be obtained from the bush, Judd would have to drag the boat across more than three kilometres of sea ice and row to Pender Harbour, a hundred-and-sixty-kilometre round trip. He was always a welcome sight at Portuguese Joe's bar in Irvines Landing and never had to pay for a drink. All you had to do was ask him how things were going.

"Could be worse. Had a hard blow and a cedar tree come down on the shack is all."

"Very big?"

"Naw, only about six foot on the butt."

"Good God, Judd. Didn't it do a lot of damage?"

"Naw. Fell crost the bed right where the old woman was sleepin', but it hung up on the stove before it could git 'er. Tore the roof off is all."

"That's terrible, Judd!"

"Naw. I just took a couple blocks off the end and split up a mess o' shakes. Old woman bin after me fer a new roof anyways."

"What about the rest of the tree. How did you remove it?"

"Didn't bother. It was pointin' in the stove anyways, so I jus' lit the fire and stuck the Gilchrist jack on the other end. Every time the old woman wanted some exter heat, I just hollered at the kid to go out and give a few clicks on the jack. It was auto-feed, like."

"So it wasn't so bad after all."

"Hell no. I got a new roof and a whole winter's heat without once havin' to leave the shack."

I sometimes wonder if it was due to Judd Johnstone that the entire Jervis Inlet–Nelson Island area seemed to become such a prime bullshit-producing zone. When I was growing up there it seemed you couldn't get a straight answer out of anybody.

Certainly you couldn't get one out of James "Mac" MacDonald, the globe-trotting American playboy who fell under the Princess's spell in 1919. "After travelling around the world and seeing many of its famous beauty spots, I felt I was well able to evaluate the magnificence of Princess Louisa," he wrote in one of his more sober utterances. "This place had to equal or better anything I had seen."

Like many another wealthy American who no sooner spied a thing of beauty in a foreign land than he had to have it, MacDonald promptly applied to the BC government to purchase the inlet head, and the government turned out to be eager to un-load it. Their appraisal of the 292-acre site, which would come to be called "The Eighth Wonder of the World" and attract twenty thousand gawkers a season despite its inaccessibility, was that only 42 acres were flat enough to be of any use, so MacDonald could have the whole thing for $420, if that wasn't asking too much. He took possession in 1927.

Through absolutely no fault of its own, this turned out to be the best thing the government could have done. Within a few years MacDonald would be turning down $400,000 offers from hotel chains and preserving the area for public use with a determination the government would not come to appreciate until 1964, when MacDonald finally had the satisfaction of seeing his beloved charge consecrated as a Class A marine park.

Rich, eloquent and handsome, Mac MacDonald could have had his pick of successful careers, but from his fateful encounter with the Princess in the prime of his life until the day he could no longer hobble around on his own, he devoted his entire existence to being her chief admirer, protector and ambassador to the world. He got married in 1939, but the new wife made the mistake of forcing him to choose between the Princess and her, and a divorce quickly followed.

Mac left the inlet only during the winter months, when the weather becomes much harsher than the coastal norm. At first he rented a *pied-à-terre* in Pender Harbour from his friend Bertrand Sinclair, a writer of popular novels about fishing, logging and cowboying, and later he established regular winter digs in Acapulco. From May to October he was back at Princess Louisa, continuing his endless study of her moods, cataloguing her wonders and expounding on them to visitors. In time every feature in the inlet, from Chatterbox Falls to Trapper's Rock, came to be known by a name Mac gave it. He became a walking encyclopedia of inlet history and lore, most of it unreliable but all of it highly entertaining.

MacDonald's presence became an attraction in itself, compelling regulars like megastar John Barrymore to return year after year

to pass long evenings lounging on the afterdeck of his splendifer-
ous MV *Infanta*, where Mac would tell stories and point out faces
in the rock formations of the bluffs. (Barrymore claimed to have
discovered Napoleon, though Mac later speculated you had to be
drinking Napoleon brandy to see it.) Hollywood types seemed to
take a particular shine to Mac. At various times he entertained the
likes of Ronald Colman, William Powell and Mack Sennett, complete with his entourage of bathing beauties, who filmed part of a
movie called *Alaska Love* in the inlet, but he was equally attentive
to locals and kids, reputedly turning down dinner with celebrity
broadcaster Arthur Godfrey so he could keep a storytelling date
at the youth camp. This is all the more notable considering Mac's
legendary appetite for free grub. It is said that from the time the
first yacht showed up in the spring to the time the last one left in
the fall, he never ate his own cooking.

MacDonald was a great admirer of Judd Johnstone and,
after Judd moved south to Hardy Island, of his brother Steve, who
stayed up-inlet all his life. He was also a great fan of old Casper.
During one of his winters south, MacDonald hired some professional musicians to make a record of Casper's songs, which proved
a great hit among inlet fanciers and netted the old smithy a rare
spot of cash. MacDonald was outraged in 1940 when aviation
tycoon Thomas Hamilton talked Casper into parting with his beloved acreage for five hundred dollars so he could build a luxury
resort called Malibu Lodge. Mac cheered when Malibu went broke
in 1947 and was taken over by Young Life, a non-denominational
church group offering low-budget vacations to city kids.

MacDonald was particularly attentive to Muriel Blanchet,
the adventuring Victoria widow who cruised the inlet with her
five children in the 1930s. With the help of Hubert Evans she
recorded her experiences in the coastal classic *The Curve of Time*,
which has a lengthy passage describing Mac as "the Man from
California," which of course he wasn't.

74

Under the inlet's influence MacDonald became one of the most ardent apostles of the creed that humanity was placed on the Sunshine Coast "not to be doing but to be." He even went so far as to dedicate himself formally to "the satisfying state of loaferhood."

"The world needs ten million full time thinking loafers dedicated to the purpose of bringing this cockeyed life back to its normal balance," he declared in his five-point manifesto of loaferdom.

Of course it helped to be the favourite son of a Seattle grocery heiress, a fact MacDonald made no bones about, advising would-be loafers: "Before birth, look the field over and pick out a family in which some member has misspent his life in amassing sufficient do-re-me to permit you to dodge the squirrel cage." In this he differs from the Johnstone boys, who would argue that you could enjoy the best the coast had to offer with no more accumulated assets than a jackknife and a box of matches.

I remember Mac as a pleasant old man with a crown of luminous silver hair who used to keep his houseboat the *Seaholm* in Madeira Park while he waited for the inlet to thaw in the spring. I had a paper route, and while it was a bit of nuisance to paddle over to where he was anchored, it was always worth seeing what nonsense he would come up with. One spring he launched into a big production about a new sport that had taken Acapulco beaches by storm that season, and ceremoniously produced this wonderful innovation he'd smuggled back just for my benefit. I was excited by the buildup but disappointed by the actual item, which looked like the lid off a small plastic garbage can. He said you flicked it so it sort of hovered like a flying saucer. He made me practise it with him until I had the knack, then commanded me to go off and spread the fad among my friends. That was how Madeira Park became the first Canadian beachhead of the Frisbee craze, away back in 1957. To a twelve-year-old, Mac seemed like nothing so much as a great big over-aged kid, which I am sure is a judgment he would have been most delighted to accept. The only thing you had to watch was that he didn't lure you inside his cabin and try to make you play chess. As a chess fanatic he was known for his willingness to play with anyone, no matter how incompetent, but I am sad to say even his legendary patience was checkmated in my case.

Mac died in a Seattle rest home in 1978. His ashes are planted inside a boulder at the head of Princess Louisa, beneath an inscription that reads LAIRD OF THE INLET, GENTLEMAN, FRIEND TO ALL WHO CAME HERE.

III.

On These
Accordioned
Shores

The Kleins and Their Dale

Kleindale is a place that doesn't appear on any map. You can drive through it and not see its name on a single sign. Still, there is something about the place that catches the visitor's attention, something a little different. After winding its way past miles of bluffs and rocky shores, the Sunshine Coast highway branches into a gentler landscape where there are open fields, fallen-down dykes and fences, a classic hip-roofed barn, a straggling cow or two. The shore is a muddy estuary, and the streams that cascade down the wall of the Caren Range beyond this small green valley here meander turbidly through a salt marsh and a long tidal flat decorated with gleaming mounds of oyster shells. The perceptive eye will detect signs of mighty pioneering effort all around this small valley, from the great notched tree stumps that stud the foothills like monuments to an earlier time when survival depended on physical strength and determination, to the road that scrawls up the sheer face of the mountain, ending in a caved-in mine that speaks of almost depraved industry, to the little graveyard tilted toward the sea where many of the wooden crosses bear the surname Klein. To those slumbering souls it must seem as though their enemies have finally triumphed, have finally succeeded in erasing their hard-won mark from the history of Canada. Fortunately, one of their descendants has gone to the trouble of capturing their story in a book called, appropriately, *The Little Green Valley* and has created a record that will prove harder to erase.

It was different when I was growing up in Pender Harbour back in the 1950s. The Kleins were very much a force to be reckoned with and Kleindale was their turf. Nobody would have dared write a tell-all book like this in those days, lest several hulking loggers appear at one's doorstep offering to set matters right in the way they knew best—by physical force. Luckily our author, Ray Phillips, is a chip off the old block himself, his mother having been a second-generation Klein, and although he was chided in his youth for only being "half a Klein" that is more Klein than almost anyone else around here can lay claim to these days.

Ray says he was aware as a kid that the rest of the coast viewed Kleindale as hillbilly territory, referring to it behind its back as "Dogpatch"—a reference to the popular comic strip of the day featuring the Ozarkian antics of Li'l Abner and his tribe. I will admit I was party to this sentiment as a youngster growing up in Pender Harbour, although it would be hard to find a more laughable case of the pot calling the kettle black. Kleindale was undoubtedly the haunt of some of the area's more haywire characters but also some of the area's more substantial citizens, including the cultured Bun Forrester, the unofficial "Mayor of Pender Harbour"; George Southwell, a renowned painter whose bare-bosomed murals decorated the rotunda of the provincial legislature until they were covered up in a fit of political correctness many years later; Dorothy Klein, who became Queen of the New Orleans Mardi Gras; and the statesmanlike John Cline (sic), surely the only Sunshine Coast inhabitant ever to operate a successful stable of racehorses at the Santa Anita racetrack in Los Angeles.

The original Kleins, Frederick and Martina, were German immigrants who had crossed the United States and ended up on a pioneer ranch in Surrey, BC. The clan was hot-blooded from the start: Mrs. Klein's mother had shot her husband dead and Frederick shot one of his own sons in a drunken rage—a case of apparent filicide revealed for the first time in Ray's book. This latter event resulted in the couple's permanent separation, which took place in Surrey before either of them moved to Kleindale, but before that unfortunate event they had been happy enough together to produce ten children: Bill (1882), Fred (1884), George (1886), Minnie (1887), Charlie (1892), Florence (1896), John (1889), Mabel (1901), Mary (1906) and Pete (1909). Most spent portions of their lives in Kleindale and raised families there, populating a whole community almost by themselves. Another Kleindale resident, Oliver Dubois, told Ray he went to a dance at the local school and got into one of the unavoidable fights but couldn't knock his opponent down because Kleins were so thick on the ground there was no space to fall over. After naming all the Kleins he could remember being present—Bill Klein, Dick Klein, Pete Klein, Norman Klein, Harold Klein, Bill Klein Jr.—he opined, "I think even Klein Klein was there." It did seem like a Klein epidemic at times.

Ray's book is partly the story of his now-scattered clan and partly the story of the homely little community they and their neighbours forged out of dirt, hope and hard labour in the midst of the Great Depression. There was Ray's uncle Charlie, reputedly the strongest man on the coast, who liked to spend his days courting beer parlour queens and composing folk songs, some now graduated into coastal legend; Earl Laughlin, the ex-rum-runner who had such a way with animals he even taught his cow to do tricks; Dave Gibb, the exiled son of a Scottish laird who lived in a tarpaper shack and survived by hunting cougars; "Sis" Harris, the lady boss logger who took no guff; Ronald Heid, the six-foot-seven giant who was as strong as an ox and just as smart; and my favourite, Fred Sutherland, "the world's dirtiest butcher."

The Little Green Valley is an unpretentious book about a community so modest its own founding families abandoned it with barely a backward glance, but after reading it you will never be able to drive past the empty fields of Kleindale without sensing them full of ghosts.

Libraries under Fire

Recently I had the unsettling experience of chairing a Writers' Union panel on the future of libraries. The expert consensus was that since you can now store the entire Western canon on a thumb drive, there is no longer any need for large buildings on prime real estate stuffed with musty books. I appreciate the cold logic of such claims but I think they miss something.

Libraries have quite a history here on the Sunshine Coast. The Sechelt Public Library recently celebrated its fiftieth anniversary, having started as a centennial project, but it is a mere babe compared to the Gibsons Library, which started in 1914. It's instructive to think that in a settlement with no medical clinic, no bank, no curling rink, no financial advisers, no spas and very little indoor plumbing, someone had nevertheless felt the need to start a library.

It's even more amazing for me personally to think this book thing has been going on that long because I came to the coast in 1950 and it was years before I saw anyone reading a book. It might have been different if I lived in the sophisticated south end, but alas I was confined to the underprivileged north end.

Actually our logging camp did have one book.

Our family owned it and until the age of eight it was the only book I knew. It was called *The Great Controversy between Christ and Satan*. My parents weren't churchgoers, but their parents had been churchy enough to do for the next three generations and my father inherited *The Great Controversy* when Gramma Boley died. The Boleys had owned a large spread in the Fraser Valley and a lot of people in her place would have been tempted to will the land to her kids when she died, but Gramma was a woman of rare principle so she willed it to evangelist Phil Gaglardi's radio crusade. Instead of 160 acres of prime real estate we got *The Great Controversy between Christ and Satan*. It was a loving gesture to her way of thinking because that land was worth a lot of money and who knows what kind of sinful ways it might have led us into. And there was no way around it, *The Great Controversy* was a handsome book. It had tooled leather covers and gilt edging. It held a place of prominence in our cookhouse between the pile of old *Hiballer* magazines and the box of used sparkplugs. Everybody who came by ended up hauling it down at one time or another, probably hoping it might contain nude paintings of Greek goddesses, or maybe medical illustrations of female anatomy. Alas, the most exciting imagery it offered was the psychedelic marbling on the endpapers. Dad used to refer to it as "the hundred-thousand-dollar book" and I thought it really was a precious heirloom. It was years before I realized the full weight of his bitterness.

To me the most interesting thing about that book was it had an actual bookworm in it which was diligently honeycombing the leather spine. It must have been lonely work. I'm sure he was the only bookworm of any kind up on the north end of the coast, for all that they had already been flourishing for forty years down at the Gibsons end.

Coming from such a bookless background it has been interesting to watch the whole coast evolve into such a nest of bibliophiles. It seems every time I venture out of doors these days someone runs up to me to ask what I think of all this horrid talk about electric books, often clutching an old-style "legacy" book to their bosom as if they feared some technology proponent might try to sneak up and wrest it away.

I don't think they have to worry. When archaeologists of the distant future are sifting the ashes of our civilization shaking their heads at the appalling idiocies that finally brought about our demise, one thing I am sure will loom large on the positive side of the ledger will be our love and respect for books. I grant the digital wizards all their arguments that ebooks are cheaper, fly through the air with the greatest of ease and can indeed be read in the bath if you purchase the ninety-nine-dollar RainEread™ accessory. But so what?

Things as deeply entrenched in our psyches as books don't disappear overnight just because some propeller-head comes along and announces he's made a better mousetrap. If that were so, painting would have stopped the minute photography was invented. Instead we have more art galleries than at any time in history and a painting of someone having a bad day selling for $120 million. Sailboats didn't disappear the minute the Easthope brothers announced their first marine engine. A ferry trip across Howe Sound on any sunny summer day will confirm there's more rag-hangers afloat than ever, no matter they spend 99 per cent of their time motoring. Bicycles were supposed to disappear at the appearance of the first motor car. Horses, too. I read somewhere there are more horses in BC today than there were in 1900, and they are living much happier lives. Dogs and cats were first domesticated for very practical purposes and I can show you vet bills to prove they account for a much larger share of the GDP now than when they actually earned their keep. When you think about it, we are surrounded by things that once we only kept out of dull practicality but we now keep because we darnwell feel like it. The very fact books and libraries have become obsolete may mean their best years are just beginning.

Pete the Poet

In 1972 when my wife Mary and I started publishing local writers I asked our mentor Lester Peterson, author of *The Gibson's Landing Story*, if we should look up Peter Trower, a poetry-spouting logger known in coastal camps as "Pete the Poet." I thought as lifelong Gibsonians for sure they would be friends.

"My advice is to stay away from him," Les said. "No good writing ever came from lying around drinking and doing drugs."

In 1972 there was probably nothing Les could have said that would have piqued my interest more and I looked Pete up at the first opportunity.

I've seen the writing bug bite some unlikely people, and Pete was one of the unlikeliest. He lived in a little shack in his mother's backyard that was for all the world like a typical logging camp bunkhouse, right down to the mouldy socks and stale beer aroma. An army cot across one end served as Pete's bed, sofa, desk and pulpit. It was piled with papers and thick binders of unpublished writings. A low table occupied the centre of the tiny room, a battered portable typewriter on the end nearest Pete. Shelves around the edges were stuffed with books, records and an impressive row of diaries bound in uniform red covers, which Pete kept meticulously.

Pete was a strange enough apparition himself. He was in his early forties then, getting toward the end of the best years for the type of logger he was, a rigging slinger, which meant he scrambled around in the logging slash as a kind of playing coach to the rigging crew that hooked the cables onto the logs to yard them down to the trucks—hard and dangerous work. He was medium-sized and solidly built with a strangely smooth, almost feminine complexion, which stayed with him until his dying days. He was bald but kept the fact secret by wearing a flat, Ben Hogan–type cap during all waking hours. Except for a brief period when a wealthy patron fitted him with a wig, he was never seen bareheaded in public.

"Hey, man, it's about time you came by. I was startin' to think you maybe heard some bad stories about me," Pete chuckled without getting up from the cot. He had a way of gurgling his words from the back of his throat as if he was only half sure about letting them out, a habit that earned him the nickname "Mumbles" in school. His speech was a unique mix of coastal logger slang and '50s street jive, a hangover from the Vancouver zoot-suit scene he'd flirted with in his teens.

"Wanna brew?" he asked, holding up his half-empty stubby. The druggie rap was overstated in Pete's case—he'd done thirty days in Oakalla Prison for possession of a pipe containing minute traces of cannabis but he was only an occasional toker. The drinking part however was all too true. That he lived to age eighty-seven is a testament to the human liver. We soon worked through the half case stashed under his bunk and made our way up to the old Pen Hotel where I left him in the care of friends about six hours later (Pete never learned to drive, which was a good thing). Again and again during that afternoon he'd turn to me, stick out his jagger-scarred paw and say, "We're partners, okay? I'll put my whole weight behind this *Raincoat Chronicles* and we'll blow the lid off this joint." I wasn't quite sure what I was getting into. If Les Peterson was right, it was probably nothing more than idle talk.

89

But Les was wrong. With a willing outlet for his writing, Pete quit the woods and over the next twenty years that little bunk shack became a veritable writing factory. Between hangovers Pete turned out fifteen books of poetry, hundreds of articles, first for *Raincoast Chronicles,* then other magazines, and three novels. Some of his poems from that time, like "The Alders," "Along Green Tunnels" and "The Last Spar Tree on Elphinstone Mountain," are certified BC classics. Before passing to the great bunkhouse in the sky, Pete the Poet lived to have the mayor of Vancouver proclaim a special "Peter Trower Day" and saw his name cemented into the literary walk of fame outside the Vancouver Library, not to mention posted on Trower Lane in his hometown of Gibsons. He is the only Sunshine Coast writer to be so honoured, and certainly the only ex-rigging slinger.

The Unlikely Cannabis Guru

As you reach a certain age you begin to get used to seeing your contemporaries bite the dust. Some make you feel bad because you don't feel badly enough about them. Others make you feel bad for not being able to get over it. Mike Poole fits the latter category for me. He died several years back now, but every time I think of him I get this raw feeling. A guy as vital as Mike deserved more time.

I first got to know Mike properly around 1974 when our mutual friend and fellow Sunshine Coast lifer Pete Trower published his first book of logging poems, *Between the Sky and the Splinters*, through my fledgling company.

Mike was by this time a well-established producer with CBC TV and he announced he wanted to make a film of *Between the Sky and the Splinters*. I didn't know much at the time, but I knew this was a highly unusual notion. A film based on a book of poetry? I was quite proud of *BTSATS* and secretly felt it was fated to win the Nobel Prize despite the fact the hippie artist who had designed it made it the size of a kids' picture book and set the entire text in italic, goofy effects that were not helped by my ink-splattered self-taught pressmanship. Nevertheless I was convinced the unlikeliness of a gat-toothed, beer-swilling logger writing quite fine poetry would turn heads and was a little suspicious that this film guy from the city wanted in on our action. Mike was at this time one of the top documentary makers in the country, whose work always showed in prime time and set off regular political uproars. He directed *The Beachcombers* and started *The Nature of Things* with David Suzuki. His hour-long documentary *Tankerbomb* deserves much credit for the still-controversial moratorium on tanker traffic along the BC coast and *Island of Whales*, starring Gregory Peck, helped bring about the worldwide moratorium on whaling. He'd won every award from a Gemini (Canada's Oscar) to a British Wildscreen, the Olympic Gold Medal of nature films.

According to Mike, he only wanted to help Pete. They'd been friends growing up in Gibsons before Pete got sidetracked into the hard-drinking life of the camps and now that Pete had managed to publish a book, Mike wanted to treat him to half an hour of prime network time as a vote of confidence. But looking back, I realize Mike was also seeking something in the project for himself—a chance to get back to his own roots and do something more personally meaningful than current affairs on CBC.

I know this because not many years later, Mike astounded the film world by quitting the business to write his own books about the coast. First there was *Ragged Islands,* about his thousand-kilometre canoe trip down the coast. Then there was *Romancing Mary Jane,* about his season as an ill-fated marijuana farmer. It is ironic that, out of all the things he did, that naughty little memoir is what he will be remembered for.

To me Mike's emergence as a cannabis guru came with a large dollop of irony because the Mike I had known was a very straight, slightly naive dude who could be counted on to stay sober and steer the boat while everybody else got wasted. In fact I think I saw him smoke his first joint. It was on Pete's film shoot. Somebody handed him a good-sized spliff adequate for the whole film crew and he said, "Oh, thanks," and proceeded to smoke the whole thing himself, winding up rolling on the floor speaking in tongues. It was curious to see him, a few years later, touring the country as a marijuana expert and I wondered if it was something he had deliberately done to try to shake that square-shouldered, clear-eyed persona he had carried with him since birth. After the marijuana episode he became quite a bit more colourful himself.

With great foresight he bought a choice piece of Middlepoint waterfront when ordinary mortals could still afford it and throughout the 1990s he and his second wife Carole set about building their dream home, Mike doing much of the fine finishing himself. Once he was securely ensconced back on the coast, he set about his great project, a novel about his childhood in Granthams Landing. He set it during ww i instead of ww ii, but that clean-limbed country boy who falls for the rich city girl is unmistakably the young Mike. It didn't do as well as he had hoped, probably because he went into too much detail about every aspect of old-style coast life from tuning up an Easthope engine to rigging a wooden spar tree, but he was content to have finally arrived in the exact place he wanted to be doing the exact thing he wanted to do. As he wrote in a biographical note not long before his death, "What next? Another book, I expect, though I'm not sure what. And in fact, the subject is less important than the activity. Not to be writing seems, for me at least, to be less than fully alive."

Few pursued the goal of being fully alive as restlessly as Mike, and that is why it seems so unfair that having chased his dream all the way around the world to the place he started out, he had so little time to enjoy it.

Echoes of the Great War

All through the years 2014 to 2018 official Canada busily turned out programs and speeches trying to make something of the centenary of the outbreak, then the milestone battles, then the end, of World War I, but it was hard work getting the masses excited about an event so distantly obscured in the mists of time. Jack Babcock, the last centenarian centurion who served in that sad mud-and-blood-spattered conflict, finally faded away in 2010 at the age of 109 and for many people the events of 1914–18 now seem to have migrated into the history books alongside Waterloo and Trafalgar and all that roster of memorable mayhem that exists on paper only.

Here on the Sunshine Coast there was one connection to 1914 that ended up being celebrated in song and story, including an entire novel by the late Mike Poole, but it didn't take place in the Somme, it took place on the side of Mount Elphinstone. As the war wore on and initial enthusiasm for defending the Empire was undercut by reports of blundering generals wasting hundreds of thousands of lives in muddy screw-ups, many men thought better of enlisting and headed for the hills. The Elphinstone draft dodgers' camp became well established and was itself the site of a famous screw-up that ended with one spooked dodger shooting another by mistake. For decades Gibsonians indulged in a community conspiracy to keep that backwoods killing from official attention, but memories of it have also died with fading memories of the era.

It ought to be different for me because until 2015 I was privileged to talk daily to a man whose life formed a living link to that time, but my dad, Frank White, who was born on May 9, 1914, could be forgiven for not remembering too much about the actual start of the war since he was only three months old at the time. He was four by the war's end however, and a vague awareness of the war seeped into his childish consciousness.

Along with war, disease was one of the main things on parents' minds in those pre-medicare days when children under five made up 35 per cent of all Canadian deaths. The idea that the myriad diseases plaguing the young were caused by something called germs had only recently become popular and *germs* was quite the buzzword, especially when parents were urging small boys to refrain from eating dirt and kissing dogs. To a budding brain struggling to make sense of the world around him, germs seemed invisible terrorists behind no end of nasty work. And when the grown-ups weren't decrying the subversive efforts of vague, unseen forces called germs, they were decrying the foul deeds of another pervasive and equally unseen enemy called Germans. Is it any wonder little Frankie became confused by the similar-sounding words and spent ww i assuming germs and Germans were the same thing, or at least two closely allied villains?

My father's main ww i memory is a curious one. In the winter of 1918, the last year of the war, his family was living in a rural part of the Fraser Valley outside what is now Aldergrove, when the weather gods conspired to bring about that beautiful but destructive combination of rain and freezing temperatures called a "silver thaw." In this rare situation, raindrops remain liquid as long as they are in motion but the instant they hit anything solid they freeze. If the thing they hit is a tree limb, they quickly coat it in a thick jacket of ice whose weight builds until the limb snaps off with a loud bang. In 1918 so many limbs were shearing off around the White homestead it sounded like an artillery barrage. My father's father carried him out on the porch to witness the once-in-a-lifetime phenomenon, saying in his typical teasing way, "Listen, Bud! The Germans are coming!"

As we now know, enlightened parents aren't supposed to play these kinds of mind tricks on small children. Their tender minds are having a hard enough time trying to make sense of a bewildering world without mischievous adults making it harder for them. Little Frankie was left not knowing if their home was about to be blasted flat or they were all going to get a world-class case of diarrhea.

His next memory connected to the war was from Abbotsford, where the White family moved in 1919. In their zeal to honour the town's thirty-four war dead, city fathers erected an impressive twenty-foot-high obelisk—right in the centre of the town's busiest intersection. Their patriotism had obviously got the better of their practical judgment, and the effect was to turn that intersection into a kind of memorial battleground. As Dad remembered, "There weren't too many Saturday nights that went by without some drunk trying to wind his jalopy around that cenotaph." He admitted to thumping it once himself with his vintage Indian motorcycle, although he blamed loose gravel rather than strong drink for that. Eventually the city fathers decided to put an end to this undignified pummelling of the sacred symbol and in 1929 the memorial was retired to a less travelled location.

No doubt my father had many more memories about the time of the Great War and its aftermath, but over the years they faded until all he was left with was that recollection of that day standing on the porch in Aldergrove with booming and crashing on all sides. He had no way of knowing the simulated battle noise was caused by a rare quirk of weather and his father's little joke continued to puzzle him until late in life, when he stumbled across a chance reference to "the great Fraser Valley ice-storm of 1918" and was finally able to figure out exactly what was going on that day, some ninety years after the fact.

It makes the events of 1914 seem a little closer when you think of it as the time it took a boy to get his father's joke.

The Music Bug

Nobody on my side of the family could carry a tune in a wheel-barrow. My father loved to sing, but we didn't love to hear him. It sounded like Muggs the bulldog the time he ate too many spawned-out humpback salmon. And when we kids tried our own voices out in private, we discovered to our dismay that we had inherited our father's vocal talent.

Once an unwary visitor tried to get us singing Christmas carols. We got the words down okay but the actual singing produced an effect like the noise a herd of sea lions make when their sunbathing is disrupted by a boatful of shutterbugs.

The only musical instrument in the house where I grew up was a windup record player with a dwindling supply of too-breakable 78-RPM records, although I have to say it was adequate to our needs. The needle got broken on the first day but we soon learned how to improvise a replacement by doctoring a straight pin. My mother latched onto an album of *Reader's Digest Timeless Classics* at a yard sale and even though the pin made the Boston Pops string section sound like Arthur Fiedler was playing a comb, those tinny renditions of the "Flight of the Bumblebee" and "The March of the Sardar" still came through well enough to make me a confirmed believer in canned music.

When I first came to the coast in 1950, every fishboat and bunkhouse had an accordion stowed away somewhere. That—not the fiddle or guitar—was the wet coast instrument of choice. And those old squeezeboxes got lots of exercise, because there was nothing else. And it didn't matter that Parky Higgins's playing was so enthusiastic you couldn't exactly tell if he was attempting "The Beer Barrel Polka" or "On Top of Old Smokey," it was better than listening to the light plant backfire. Or at least it was different. But as soon as records came along, then eight-tracks, and you could choose between Parky and the Boston Pops, well, the rationale for learning how to make your own hokey music pretty much went out the window to my way of thinking. Like a lot of people, I figured it would only be a matter of time before live music pretty much disappeared, at least at the amateur level.

I was happy enough with this smug conclusion until I married into a family that does have the musical gene, just as plainly as the Whites don't. My wife Mary's family all play one instrument or another, some several. Her aunt Mabel was the family celebrity. She demoed Hammond organs at Eaton's Department Store. Mary joined the school band at an early age thinking it would boost her popularity. It didn't but she found it full of kids just as nerdy as her and made such good friends she still hangs out with one or two survivors fifty years later. Bands form bonds.

When Mary first made that brave and reckless decision to cast her lot with mine and gave up the cultured society of Mission, BC, for the accordioned shores of the Sunshine Coast back in the 1970s, one of the things that saved her from distraction (and me from bachelordom) was her discovery that while it lacked most of the attributes of cultured society, the coast did have a small core of musical nerds who regularly got together to play their high school band instruments. At first she joined a group called the Harbour Lights that played big-band jazz, somewhat shakily at first, then well enough to be booked for the occasional paying gig, once as far away as Powell River. Then she graduated to the Coast Symphony Orchestra and the Suncoast Concert Band. At one point she was playing in all three as well as another ensemble that accompanied Lynn Vernon's musical theatre productions and she was away so much I was wondering if the local musical scene had saved me from bachelordom or delivered me a musical form of it.

Of course, given my devotion to tailor-made stuff I was somewhat mystified by this practice of playing live music. Why bother, when you can hear Zamfir with the punch of an eight-track? Also, I'd read about musicians' loose morals and wondered if I should be worried about all the late nights my attractive young spouse was spending away from the family nest. I asked her what they did for fun.

"We play music," she said.

"Don't you talk?" I asked.

"We can't talk, we've got instruments in our mouths," she said.

"What about between pieces?"

"We really can't talk then. We have to keep quiet and listen to the conductor."

This sounded suspicious to me, and for a time I became a member of the "band widows," the non-playing spouses who followed the bands around helping set up the music stands and bulk up the audience on slow nights, but I found signs of loose living disappointingly rare. In fact I found the living torturously slow. I guess it's tolerable to listen to the same piece over and over if you are playing it, but even the "Pirates of Penzance Overture" loses some its zip after the twentieth or thirtieth run-through if you're just listening at a rehearsal. If the players were having a better time than me, it was hard to tell. They seemed very serious. There was no whooping or high-fiving or other signs of ecstasy, only the occasional mutter. They just kept their eyes on their music, listened to the conductor, and when the session was over they quietly put away their instruments and went home. When I asked Mary when they had their fun she said, "When we're playing."

"It didn't look like fun from the outside," I said.

"Well, it's not fun exactly, it's music."

"Is that more fun than fun, or less?"

"It's in a class by itself."

"How about sex, is it more fun than sex?"

"Depends." I decided not to pursue that line of inquiry any further.

Since about 1984 I've been mostly a stay-at-home supporter of the Sunshine Coast music scene, but it seems to have got on without me. Between the Symphony Orchestra and the Concert Band and the Youth Orchestra and the Pender Harbour Choir, which recently celebrated its fortieth anniversary, and the Coast Recital Society and the Pender Harbour Music Society and half a dozen festivals covering every imaginable kind of music, the coast supports more live music per capita than any place north of the Mississippi Delta, technology be damned. Not so long ago Canadian literary icon Margaret Atwood wrote an opera about famed Mohawk poet Pauline Johnson where the lead was performed to widespread acclaim by the mezzo-soprano Rose-Ellen Nichols, who just happens to be a descendant of that accordion abuser of my childhood, Parky Higgins. It's all pretty amazing when you think about it.

Novice Writer at Ninety-Nine

My papa, Frank White, was ninety-nine when he published his first book. *Milk Spills and One-Log Loads: Memories of a Pioneer Truck Driver* is a kind of book that doesn't usually get written and not just because its author was closing in on the century mark. Dad was not the sort of guy who would normally consider his life worth writing about. I don't think he ever would have got the notion into his head if not for a trick I played on him back in 1972 when he was only fifty-eight and I was only twenty-seven.

I was trying to write an article about the rise of BC coast truck logging for my fledgling history magazine *Raincoast Chronicles*, and turned to Dad for help. Like most young people I didn't give my father much credit for knowing anything but I had sat through enough of his tales to know he had been in the trucking game early on and might at least be able to give me the names of some truly important figures that I could look up.

"Jeez, How, there's a lot of jaws been broken over the question of where and when trucks first got into the woods—hell, they can't even settle on where the first logging railroad was, and trucks are a lot harder to keep track of than trains," he mused in his typical way. "I'd hafta say though, if I had to give you one name it would be old Bill Schnare ..."

I'd heard the stories about old Bill before and never gave them much credit, but now I got a crazy idea. What if we printed

Dad's take on truck logging history just the way he said it, in his own sidehill lingo? It doesn't seem all that daring now, but Barry Broadfoot had not then written his bestselling oral histories of the Great Depression and the Second World War and the idea of letting a regular guy whose only qualification to talk about an industry was having worked in it for thirty years, and especially letting him speak in the words he would use on the job talking to his fellow workers, was untrod ground as far as I knew. It also never occurred to Dad that his experiences were worth recording by themselves. He only thought they might give me leads so I could go to the Royal BC Museum and consult the official record—which I had already discovered had nothing to say about the origins of truck logging, or anything about truck logging as a historical development. There was plenty on handlogging, ox logging, horse logging, railroad logging, but nothing on truck logging. We didn't know it at the time, but we were in the act of pioneering the study of truck logging, just as he had pioneered actual truck logging. Dad loved to talk about his experiences and was unused to finding me such a willing listener. I didn't dare tell him that I was planning to print his memories word for word for fear he would clam up. My heart was in my mouth as I sent his uncut man-in-the-street reflections to the printer illustrated with his own snapshots of impossibly huge logs on sagging little trucks no bigger than modern delivery vans, worried how he and the reading public would respond.

I had good reason, as it turned out. When the logging issue of *Raincoast Chronicles* hit the streets in 1973, Dad was beyond shocked. People in those pre–social media times passed their whole lives without seeing their names in print and odd as it may seem in today's world, they didn't *want* to see their names in print. Exposure spooked them. On top of that, Dad was worried his old trucking cronies would think he was showing off and stop speaking to him. He stopped speaking to me. For a while there, I would have done anything to take back the story.

What saved my butt was the rest of the world's reaction. The logging issue of *Raincoast Chronicles* got a ton of ink and sold ten thousand copies. Every reviewer singled out Dad's verbatim reminiscences as the highlight. "How It Was with Trucks" was excerpted in magazines across Canada and has become a fixture quoted in almost every history written about the BC lumber industry since. Dad became an overnight expert, sought by researchers not just on the origins of truck logging but on every aspect of the forest industry and occasionally even on unrelated things like the value of the monarchy. In November he was invited to the BC Media Club where Mayor Art Phillips presented him with a thousand-dollar prize for Best Magazine Feature of the year. He began talking to me again, but for a long time he checked around for concealed tape recorders first.

Of course many of the reviewers and readers of the celebrated article suggested Dad keep on and write up more of his memories, and at first he pooh-poohed the idea, but after a while I realized he was quietly doing just that. He never fully admitted he was writing a book, only "fritzing around with some of the old yarns." This went on for decades. Finally I managed to raid his computer and printed up the results of all that fritzing. It filled a thousand pages and added up to 180,000 words—three times as long as the average novel.

"What the hell is all this?" he said, staring at the tall stack of paper when I delivered it to him. He had only read it in bits and hadn't seen it all connected up before.

"This is the book you've been writing for the last forty years," I said.

"Ha! I wasn't writing any book. I was just trying to jot down a few of the old yarns …"

His response on reading it all through for the first time was a bit alarming.

"I can't believe a man's life can be made so small," he said.

"What do you mean?"

"This barely scrapes the surface. There is so much more that needs to be said."

"Holy cow, it's already longer than *War and Peace*."

In the end we managed to persuade him to let go of the first part of his story, covering from his birth at the start of ww i up to the end of ww ii, which filled a sturdy volume by itself. We called that one *Milk Spills and One-Log Loads.* That went over well enough that we were able to persuade him to publish the second part the following year when he was one hundred which he gave the title, *That Went by Fast: My First Hundred Years.* I guess when it takes you four decades to jot down a few yarns, time does seem to scamper along. But now that he is gone, along with that whole world of big trees and small trucks when people lived lives that were truly private, I am ever so glad I tricked him into doing it.

Bard of the Woods

In 2017 I got to go to two writers' festivals in one summer. Our own of course, the Sunshine Coast Festival of the Written Arts, which just seems to get better every year, but also one in Whistler, where I was allowed to parade around for a few days wearing an author's badge. This happens every so often when somebody putting together a literary program decides to chuck in something for the lowbrows and I always gratefully accept. I especially enjoy the part after the reading when they ask you who your literary models are.

I always tell them Panicky Bell. Of course they don't get the joke because they've never heard of Panicky Bell. Once upon a time, when it was still acceptable to have logger sports at the PNE, the trophy for best all-round logger was called the Panicky Bell trophy. Senator Pat Carney, when she was still a lowly scribe on the *Vancouver Sun,* had held a contest to find the greatest BC logger of all time and the readers chose Panicky Bell. He'd worked all over the coast and clawed his way up to superintendent or "push" at some of the big railroad camps like Rock Bay on Johnstone Strait.

Panicky never actually wrote anything down, except log counts. His literary works live on solely in the form of beer parlour legend.

Most of the bush apes gained their reputations by jumping off the tops of spartrees and such, but Panicky's feats were all performed with the English language. Once the hiring agency in Vancouver sent up a dumb high rigger who took so long to climb his first spartree everybody on the crew knew before he reached the top Panicky would be firing him and sending him out on the next plane. When he finally got the top chopped off and paused for a breath before climbing the 150 feet back down to the ground, Panicky yelled up to him, "Hey, can you see Vancouver from up there?" The guy peers off into the fog and yells down, "Gee, no I can't Mr. Bell." Panicky yells back, "Well, you'll see 'er tomorrow."

He never fired a man with a straight line. The men used to speculate that some obvious candidates for his attention were getting a few days' reprieve while Panicky thought up an appropriate phrase to dispatch them with.

This one particular story was told to me by Peter Blue Cloud, a Mohawk from Akwesasne who did a spell working for Panicky at North Coast Camp in what was known then as the Queen Charlotte Islands, and he swore it was mostly true. WW II was still on and the wartime years were especially tough on Panicky because men were so hard to get you had to do everything you could to hang onto them, even the bad ones, and Panicky's verbal skills weren't nearly as effective in this direction. He had worked hard to assemble a decent crew and he kept a jealous watch over them because talent was so hard to replace. This paid off in a few dividends not normally found in most camps, including the odd sniff of booze over the weekend.

This one day the bunch was sitting around the bunkhouse sampling, among other things, Dawes Black Horse Ale, which came in a green bottle with a picture of a black horse on the cap. As the day progressed and the booze supply diminished, Panicky's prize donkey puncher, One-Eyed Alec Ross, started to get the idea it was time to go to town to get his teeth fixed. No self-respecting old-time logger ever went to town for any other reason. It was never to get his ashes hauled or to tie on a good thumping drunk, it was always to get his teeth fixed, although mostly the teeth rusted out without ever being seen by a dentist. So when Panicky dropped by to sample some Black Horse ale himself, Ross began explaining his sudden urgent need of dental work. Old Panicky ranted and raved and told him he couldn't go for at least three more weeks, when they would be moving trackside to another setting and there'd be a natural break in the action. Panicky took his leave, and Ross, after a few more ales, took out his glass eye and slammed it down on the iron bedframe, breaking it in two. On Bell's next pass through, Ross said, "Hey Panicky, I gotta go to town now, I just broke my eye."

"The hell you don't," Panicky said, "all we gotta do is send to town and have them ship one up on the Tuesday boat."

"No, no, that won't work," Ross said, "you have to get it fitted special by the eye doctor."

"All you gotta do is send down to where you usually get your eyes, they got your size," Panicky says.

"Maybe they could get the size, but they'd never get the colour right," Ross says. "They have to have my other eye there to match it."

"Hell, send for a dozen assorted colours, and get them to throw in a couple bloodshot ones for when you're hung over," Bell growls.

Ross kept insisting that he had to go to town for a custom fit, and besides there was all that dental work to be done. Cursing, Panicky picked up a Black Horse Ale cap off the floor and held it out to Ross.

"Here, plug this in that knothole of yours till we finish the setting, then I'll take you to town myself and buy you a whole gunny sack full of eyes."

North Coast Camp is long gone, along with the great spruce forest that was its reason for being, but Panicky Bell's unscripted lines live on.

So You Think You Had a Bad Trip on the Ferry?

There's no pastime on the Sunshine Coast more popular than kvetching about the ferries, and never have the ferries obliged us with more juicy material to work with. Still, anguished tales about risking life and limb and heavy fines to arrive by the posted sailing time only to be told ticket sales were frozen ten minutes earlier don't stand up to some of the horror stories veteran ferry riders get into, like the time in 2003 when the *Queen of Surrey*'s engine room caught fire and the car deck got so hot it melted tires.

I let the quidnuncs jabber on, because I know nobody can top the story I have up my sleeve, which has the unusual advantage of being perfectly true.

It was a rainy day in October 1959. We were coming back from our winter supply run to Vancouver and way points in our all-purpose family vehicle, a three-ton 1949 Ford gravel truck. In front were me, my little sister Cindy, my mum and my dad. In the back were two sacks of spuds, a side of beef, quite a lot of used building supplies from Jack's Junk, some belated back-to-school supplies and the tilt ram off my dad's front-end loader.

At that time Dad was bringing in the family bacon with an antique 1951 Lull bucket loader and earlier that week had lowered the bucket over a boulder, bending the ram like a horseshoe. This was serious, because there was no spare bacon in the larder and no way of getting any with a bent ram. This necessitated a run into

Vancouver, the nearest place where there was a big enough lathe to put the pretzelled part true. Then, since we were in town anyway, it was decided to stop by Woodward's, slide over to the slaughter-house, surprise the rellies, etc.

Three days later, we were rushing for the 5:30 sailing out of Horseshoe Bay, which we just squeezed aboard. Cindy, who was eleven then, was so tired she'd fallen asleep, so Mum decided to leave her in the truck while we slipped upstairs to grab a couple of Ole Elmholt's shoe-leather burgers.

This must have been the old *Quillayute*, because it had to back out from the slip and turn around, and when the skipper rang "Ahead!" the old boat would shudder and shake so madly you'd have to hang onto your coffee cup to keep it from dancing off the table. It had just finished going through this spasm when a crew-man came up to our table with a funny look on his face and asked my dad, "Did you have a truck on this boat?" Dad said we did and it was the one parked right out on the apron.

"That's what I thought," the guy said.

"Why do you ask?"

"I-I-I don't think it's there anymore," he stammered.

Naturally, our first thought was for Cindy. We tore down the stairway and by god, the truck was gone. Immediately the cry went up, *kid overboard!* The ferry stopped, lifeboats were launched, the Coast Guard was summoned and everybody lined the rails searching as we began slowly retracing our route. Mum and Dad were in the middle of having their seventeenth heart attack when Cindy ambled up rubbing her eyes wanting to know what the fuss was all about. She had woken up earlier and gone up to the washroom.

That solved one problem, but the truck was still unmistak-ably missing. There was no hope of a comeback there. They found some of our packages floating right around the place where the boat did its dancing pirouette and it was pretty clear what had happened. In their haste they hadn't blocked our wheels and when the boat started shimmying it waltzed the poor old overloaded Ford right into the drink. This was a five-star disaster pretty much, but it had come so close to being so much worse we somehow felt we'd gotten off light.

BC Ferries has never been famous for pampering the travelling public, but if you want to see how nice they can be, just have a high-profile disaster that's 100 per cent their fault. We got to sit at that special table they used to have with the little brass tag saying RESERVED FOR SHIP'S OFFICERS, we got free lemon meringue pie all round and Dad got an offer from the insurance company for about three times what our entire outfit was worth, along with a friendly suggestion all members of the family avoid talking to the press. Didn't matter. The papers loved the story and made up whatever they couldn't find out. I never believed a thing I read in a newspaper ever again.

The ferry company was terribly worried and willing to do anything we wanted, including raise the truck, which was located in four hundred feet of water. Dad would have been further ahead to take the cash payout and buy a new truck, but he needed to get that ram back so he could get back to work with his loader. I don't know why he didn't just ask the divers to retrieve the ram and leave the truck down there. I suspect he was intrigued by the logistics of raising a three-ton truck from the bottom of Horseshoe Bay and wanted to see if they could really do it. It was not done easily and the truck emerged missing most of its glass and one fender. Dad got it running but afterwards it always went down the road like a crab.

Now, that's a rough trip on the ferry.

Magic in the Mountains

When Lisa Baile first proposed climbing the mountain at the head of Princess Louisa Inlet, I was noncommittal. Princess Louisa has always held a special place in my life. It is a place of magic. I have wasted a lot of time and money going places where there was supposed to be magic only to get there and feel normal. Maybe impressed, maybe moved, but not seized by the solar plexus in the way that makes your scalp prickle and leaves no doubt. Once upon a time I could experience magic several times a day, but over the years it's got harder to find until now in my seventies I am not sure I could claim an authentic sighting once a year. But one place I can always count on finding it is Princess Louisa Inlet, that Yosemite-by-the-Sea just a hop and a skip up the coast from Egmont. I am not sure exactly what it is about the combination of sheer, mile-high cliffs, cascading waterfalls and placid seas at Princess Louisa that makes it so special, but I do know I am not the only one who senses it.

You can't spend an evening in Princess Louisa without gazing up at the amazing rock wall and wondering what it would be like to be up there looking down. I had heard talk of a trail, a gruelling climb pioneered around the 1900s by the Johnstone boys, Steve and Judd, whose father, as mentioned earlier, used to send them up there with only jackknives and salt and order them not to show their faces back at the homestead for two weeks at least. Talk about tough love. For those of us who grew up around here the legend of the Johnstone boys roaming around in the alpine above Princess Louisa with only their jackknives and the shirts on their backs served as an image of hardiness and wilderness mastery that mocked our own Junior Forest Warden skills and backyard camping attempts. At a certain time in my fitter prime I had thought seriously of following the route of the Johnstone boys and getting a taste of whatever it was they found up there but as I graduated into my dotage I began to face the fact that window had probably closed. I consoled myself with thinking that I could still make occasional boat trips to Princess Louisa itself and still get a little squirt of that old-time magic, and maybe it was better I didn't mess with those mountains lest it do something to break the wonderful spell they cast upon the waters of the inlet.

Enter Lisa Baile. I first encountered Lisa as a persistent voice on the phone pitching a book about John Clarke, a relatively little-known Vancouver man who had climbed one mountain above Mission during his youth and was so inspired by the endless vista of peaks he decided there and then to spend the rest of his life climbing as many of them as he could. He did exactly that, working during the winters only as much as needed to grubstake a summer of mountaineering, then disappearing into the wilderness for months at a time, often alone. By the time he was fifty he had over six hundred first ascents—more than any climber in the world, possibly more than any who ever lived. Lisa wanted to write the story of his life and I agreed to publish it, though I had my doubts. Lisa had never written a book and some veteran journalists had already attempted to take Clarke's measure and failed. What I didn't know about Lisa was that she was herself one of BC's outstanding mountaineers and she would bring the same dogged determination to her biographical task as she had honed conquering some of BC's most daunting crags. She made every false start and went down every blind alley a beginning author could, but she just kept slogging and eventually ended up with an excellent book published in 2011 as *John Clarke: Explorer of the Coast Mountains.*

When Lisa began angling to drag me into the mountains at the head of Princess Louisa—one of which had been named in honour of John Clarke—you'd think I would have realized I was in for it. But no, I kept trying to dodge her for more than a year. I pleaded my age—but she was six years older than me and had just spent two weeks glacier-hopping in the Kitimat Range, following hard on more than three hundred kilometres of paddling down the South Saskatchewan River. I pleaded my wobbly knees—but her climbing partner Peter Paré had one artificial hip and was on the waiting list for another. I pleaded my lack of fitness after forty years of pushing paper. I didn't stand a chance.

On September 9, there we were, tied up at the Princess Louisa dock gazing up at the sun setting on the mile-high crest of the peak they call One-Eye, ten very fit, very experienced hikers and me, laying out over five hundred pounds of climbing rope, crampons, dried food, rain gear and spare underwear—but not much of that. When you're travelling with serious climbers, every sock is scrutinized. Lisa ripped through my pack—"Don't need this, don't need that … Bathing suit? You must be joking!" These pros have everything calculated to the last ounce.

I was accompanied by two co-workers from the Harbour Publishing office, Annie Boyar and Heather Lohnes, both young and fit, as well as eight expert mountaineers assembled by Lisa, and we had spent the previous day running up Jervis Inlet from Pender Harbour in my boat, the *Lisa* (no relation) *Diane.*

While trying to appear the unflappable captain, there were several items causing a slight flutter of concern in my breast. Number one of course was, would I be able to shake off the effects of forty years of pencil-pushing effectively enough to drag my wasted carcass up this rather precipitous hill? That was at the fore of everybody's mind I'm sure, and was the main reason Lisa had assembled a support team consisting of some of BC's most experienced climbers. Ed Zenger was an actual Swiss guide. John Baldwin was second only to the immortal John Clarke in the list of feats pulled off in the Coast Mountains. And Peter Paré, Lisa's long-time climbing partner, was a licensed physician. They had ropes, ice axes, those spiky things for walking on glaciers and a satellite phone to call in air support if all else failed. I had a feeling this team was ready to get me up that mountain if they had to disassemble me and carry me up in sections.

I was also worried about the boat. This goes without saying. When I am out in any boat, I am always in a state of worry. This boat was very shipshape with a new computer-controlled diesel engine, but the battery had been low when I started and should not have been. It had been plugged into a shore charger and should have been right up. But it had come up after running the engine for a few hours and now seemed fine. Still the question niggled: Why had it been down at first?

Next, we were planning to be up the hill for two or three or maybe four days and I wasn't sure you were allowed to leave a boat unattended that long at the Princess Louisa dock, owned and controlled by the private Princess Louisa Society. Fortunately, one of the first people I ran into when we tied up was the president of the society, who wanted me to reprint an old book about the inlet. Using this as a foothold, I extracted a guarantee our boat would be fine. This turned out to be problematic, but put my mind at ease for the time being.

My concerns weren't helped by the official-looking sign posted at the start of the trail saying this was not really a trail and was very dangerous and nobody should use it, and if you did the park people took no responsibility. This would have been enough to turn me back if I'd been on my own and seemed to indicate the wrong route, but to my climbing partners it was apparently a sure indication of the right one. These were people who weren't interested in a route unless it was at least off limits to ordinary, sign-obeying folks.

The hardest part of this whole trip was the next five hours of hiking from sea level to 4,700 feet, just as steep as you could stand, crawl and climb. The first hour was the worst. That was when all the joints began protesting—"Just a minute here! What do you think you're doing? We didn't sign on for this." And the lungs. They felt like they were exhaling blue flame. And the muscles. They passed through fatigue to something like agony that involved seizure, twitching and pain radiating in red waves like an Antiphlogistine ad. I kept telling myself this must be that wall I've heard about, I just have to crash through it then I will have clear sailing. So I would do that, only to discover a thicker wall waiting on the other side. I knew then that I would never make it. So I collapsed and gave up. To my relief, lean, twentysomething Heather and Annie also collapsed and gave up.

After lying moaning on the moss for fifteen minutes, a funny thing happened. All the agony went away. We began to see a further attempt as a distinct possibility, then a probability, then a darn good idea. At just the right time, the real mountaineers, who had long before climbed out of sight, reappeared without their packs, hoisted ours and disappeared up the trail laughing and unconcerned about our condition.

It was then that I had the blazing insight that saved the trip. It was not about pushing through walls at all. It was about stopping to rest when you got tired. It was about breaking the task into bite-sized chunks. And beyond that, it was about finding a pace that allowed you to last the optimum length of time between breaks. The key was to learn to ignore all pressure to keep up with anybody else and just let your own wonky body tell you how fast and far to go. Probably someone less wordy would cover this amazing breakthrough simply as finding your rhythm. Anyway, once I found it I realized I could probably climb any distance—given enough time and friendly sherpas to supply food and essentials.

Ninety per cent of a climb like that can be covered with three words: slog, slog, slog. Your head is down and your mind is locked on the task of securing the next step. There could have been a whole convention of sasquatches in Shriner hats along that trail and unless they were actually blocking the way I wouldn't have noticed. You are so fixated on the task, it is only the rest stops that end up getting noticed and photographed. One was the so-called "trapper's cabin" which is really just a heap of rotting logs beside a rather nice waterfall some of the hardier types employed as a cold shower. Another was the blueberry bog, where the advance guard was waiting with brimming measuring cups of grape-sized blueberries. I wondered where all the three-cup measuring cups came from before coming to understand real mountaineers used them as all-purpose dishware, for better scientific control of food consumption. One thing I did notice out of the corner of my eye was that the tree trunks were getting smaller and farther apart as we approached the alpine. At a place called the first campsite, where lesser teams stopped on the bank of a pleasant stream at the end of their first day, it was still treed but shortly beyond that the trees gave way to shrubs. We powered on over the 4,700-foot ridge and down into a bare granite bowl looking up at Mount John Clarke.

It is truly a different world up there. The landscape is scrubbed clean as if the glaciers had only passed through yesterday. Vegetation is restricted to crevices and it looks foreign, as if one were on a different continent. The few stunted firs that survive stand out so forlornly on the ridges they look like lonely climbers, frozen in place. The most dynamic feature of that world is the rock. It is all bare, diamond-hard granite, but it is sculpted like bread dough. Vast fields of bare granite undulate like waves. The campsite area was irregularly punctured by perfectly round holes filled with sun-warmed water, each of which soon had a grateful climber in it.

Small tarns and larger lakes glittered with clear, emerald-tinted water. And to the west we could see a Dinky Toy version of Princess Louisa, miniaturized by distance.

We spent the next day roaming around the nearer ridges admiring the crazy shapes of the glaciated granite and testing the waters of the different lakes and pools (all frigid) before setting out on our final climb up Mount J.C. on the third day. This was only about half the distance of our first climb and generally without the challenges of slithering up slimy crevices or under huge boulders. There was a small glacier to cross, but the hardest thing about that was installing and removing the crampons, the claw-like devices that attach to your boots to prevent slippage on the ice. The final ascent was a little tricky, not so much because the trail passed over a field of loose rock, but because it skirted a straight three-thousand-foot fall into the Sims Creek gorge.

It was a beautiful clear day and most of the peaks from Toba Inlet to Mount Baker were on glittering display. Hundreds of them, and the mountaineering crew had stories to tell about previous adventures on an impressive number of them. Most of the stories were about what struck me as terrible suffering due to wretched weather and unforeseen difficulty, although this seemed to be the part the tellers enjoyed telling about the most. Strange bunch, these mountaineers.

There were no hardships on this trip. The mid-September weather had cleared and reverted to mid-July temperatures. At night we lay on our backs on the sun-warmed granite and looked up at the stars, which were so bright we couldn't take our eyes off them. Alas, there was not a single person in that party of engineers, writers, doctors, researchers and Swiss guides who could positively identify anything but the Big Dipper. The next day dawned just as fair, and despite their disappointment at having no blizzards to battle, the mountaineers voted to extend the trip another day. At first I had been insistent on getting back to my pressing pre-Christmas work schedule but I was as seduced by the halcyon spell of the place as the others and agreed to stay if I could use the sat phone to notify the office.

We got the device out of its packaging, argued for about twenty minutes about how to interpret the instructions, and eventually had a staticky, gappy conversation with the office that put me at ease and allowed me to fully enjoy an extra day of lounging around swimming, hiking, stargazing and enjoying the sensation of being on a fresh new planet where everything was clean, unspoiled and free of the depredations of man.

It was a perfect trip, without a single sprain or tick bite. In fact it was too perfect. The outside world, perhaps influenced by my reputation for calamity and the perceived dangers of going up that forbidden trail, undertook to provide a disaster scenario where none was needed.

When I got back to the boat I was immediately accosted by a uniformed park ranger, who appeared ready to clap me in irons. There was a forty-eight-hour limit on dock tie-ups and we had been twice that. Furthermore, the boat had started making a funny beeping sound which had caused the ranger great alarm, and he had broken into it to check. It wasn't sinking as he feared, but he did find a printout for currents in Malibu Rapids that ended two days earlier, indicating to him our hiking party was two days over-due. He had just two hours earlier notified the RCMP, and after satisfying himself that I was me and we were all fine, he jumped in his speedboat and screamed out into the main inlet where he could get radiophone reception to call the RCMP off.

This left me with only the mystery of the beeping boat, which I traced to the fact the battery had once again gone dead. This was a mere matter of recharging with the gas generator, but it meant another day's delay. This meant we were now officially two days behind schedule back in Pender Harbour, but that is no problem for an expedition outfitted with a sat phone, right? We got it out again and I had another staticky conversation with base, informing them, as I thought, that we had a minor mechanical problem and would be one more day. Alas, what came through at the other end was merely a garbled message that we were broken down somewhere in Jervis Inlet. My poor wife Mary, who apparently placed more value on my scalp than she normally let on, spent the night in an agony of worry and when she hadn't heard anything further by mid-morning, called the Coast Guard.

By this time we were steaming merrily along in calm sun-sparkling seas off Potato Creek and were very excited to see the yellow Coast Guard Cormorant swooping low overhead.

"Somebody must be lost," I said.

"Wow, they're sure coming close," someone else said. This time they dropped some kind of a marker a few yards off our bow.

Just then our onboard radiophone burst out with "*Lisa Diane, Lisa Diane, Lisa Diane*, this is Coast Guard Cormorant XYZ-34. Please come in."

It took us forever to satisfy them that we were fine, we were not overdue according to the last ETA we had phoned in, and there was no possible way of classifying our situation as any kind of an emergency. Reluctantly as it seemed to me, they turned back the way they had come and phoned Mary to say all was well. It had only taken twenty minutes from the time she first phoned them for her to receive the all-clear.

It certainly made for a little excitement on what is normally a long, boring run down Jervis, but it still rankles a bit that even when something in my life goes perfectly, those closest to me refuse to believe it.

IV.

Nothing Can Be Too Big of a Deal If It's Happening Here

When the Cat Does Not Come Back

Friends think I'm anti-cat. I admit I haven't gone to great lengths to dispel the notion, but I would argue that has more to do with a certain mischief bone located somewhere just to the south of my funny bone that acts up when overexposed to the earnestness of some cat lovers. I can't help myself. I guess it also has something to do with my relationship to my late Jack Russell terrier, Rocky, which some people hinted was unnatural. This is also a misconception. I mean, he *liked* to help steer the car, and he *really did* appreciate my lectures on the essential role of garbage dumps. At least he didn't cover his ears or make a show of loud snoring like other members of my family. Just because a guy likes certain highly intellectual and sensitive dogs doesn't mean he has to hate cats.

I think I proved this, after Rocky passed to his reward, by not filing for divorce when Mary adopted a fluffy cat called Zorra. Zorra had been the pride of a local poetess who was moving to Europe and wanted to place her in a literary household. I admit I was influenced by the fact Zorra came with a near-new travel carrier worth at least forty dollars.

The thing about cats is they don't need my affection. They just throw themselves at the first warm body they come across and flaunt their charms until they have what they want, whereupon they stalk away looking for the next sucker. In the human species there is a word for this kind of behaviour that can't be printed in a family publication but cat people apparently find it endlessly endearing.

Rocky used to follow me from room to room and when I came back from getting the newspaper at the end of the driveway would reward me with a welcome that would make the returning Odysseus blush. Zorra only showed interest in our existence at feeding time. She would appear at the door of Mary's office on the stroke of five and let out an accusing yowl that clearly translated as, "Look, you only have one important thing to do and I shouldn't have to remind you every single day!"

I will say this about Zorra, and that is that she had a very beautiful coat. The trouble was, she wouldn't let you touch it. She would stride up purring but stop so all you could reach was the crown of her head. If you insisted on stroking her voluptuous flanks, she would lacerate your hand with a viper-quick chomp. For the first few months we went to great efforts to keep her on separate floors from our Rocky replacement, a bull-terrier cross whose jaw makes up a third of his body length and whom various websites warned would prove to be an intractable cat-killer. Inevitably, they found each other, and Rocky II didn't stop yelping for an hour. After that *he* made sure they were always on different floors.

Yes, she was a good hunter. Of beautiful songbirds and blind shrews. The fat rats who spent unmolested hours gnawing through the walls of the composter and removing insulation from hot wires throughout the house she didn't deign to notice. I suspect she regarded rats and humans as closely related.

Zorra helped me to clarify my thinking about cats. She had all the usual cat characteristics of haughty independence, but in overproof concentration. She accepted our enslavement to her whims like some visiting royal, careful never to betray the slightest hint of gratitude. I grew to have a sneaking admiration for her. Her act of untouchable superiority was so seamless, so über-confident, it was hard not to fall in line. Cats appeal to the side of us that secretly suspects we do not deserve our heady perch atop the animal kingdom and need to be put in our place—a place far below that of cats.

They say the measure of a life is how one leaves it, and Zorra's exit couldn't have been more in character. Toward the last few months she stopped grooming her gorgeous pelt and fell to merely nibbling at her pricey fish pâté, then stopped eating altogether. Veterinary science exhausted its resources (and a good bit of ours) as she continued to shed weight like a hunger striker. It was as if she had just run out of patience with this farce called existence and decided to head for the nearest exit. One morning I found her sitting by the door, which was odd, as she hadn't ventured from her fetid nest under the bed in weeks. She was unsteady on her feet and I wasn't sure she should be outside, but when I checked an hour later she was still patiently waiting. It was a rare sunny day in February, so I decided maybe a breath of fresh air wouldn't hurt her. I watched as she staggered around the corner of the house without a backward glance.

"We'll never see her again," Mary said when I told her.

She was right. This cat never did come back.

"How did you know?" I asked.

"It's what cats do," she said. "They know when their time has come."

"How do you know that?"

"I know." There was a slight catch in her voice. I left it at that. It reminded me of another truth about cats: girls get them better than guys do.

Hijacked in Mexico

I was doing all right until I saw the coconuts. They were in a messy brown jumble outside the door of our stainless steel and marble condo in Puerto Morelos, the hamlet near Cancun that likes to call itself a fishing village though its main catch these days is gringo tourist dollars.

We like Puerto Morelos. It's like being in Mexico and not being in Mexico. You can't get a meal without tortillas, but even the sketchiest thatched-roof bar is going to have Wi-Fi. We have been going for about ten years now, off and on. One year I got the bright idea of asking our two kids if they wanted to go with us.

My fellow greybeards, who are caustic enough with me for continuing to pursue full-time employment past an age where I could get away with retiring, passionately denounced this as further evidence of galloping senility.

"You're supposed to go on holiday to rest and recover, not to change diapers and break up fights," they expostulated. As usual, they completely failed to appreciate the subtlety of my thinking.

I figured there was no way my busy kids would accept my offer but I would reap copious brownie points for asking.

The younger, who with some small assistance from his partner had recently produced his first baby, replied with an enthusiastic "Yes!"

Well, that was not so bad. We had put off crossing the country to view the new arrival and this would take care of that obligation in the pleasantest way possible.

Then the elder son, whose better half was studying for a master's degree, gallantly decided to give her some unmolested time at home and signed on with his two young daughters. At the same time my sister remembered an offhand suggestion I made several springs ago and decided this would be a good year to tag along with her brood of eight children and grandchildren. Now there were going to be seventeen of us altogether, including seven kids ranging in age from eight years to eight weeks.

Suddenly our peaceful getaway had transformed from a boringly placid retreat into a scary experiment in intergenerational family dynamics. My friends were threatening to disbar me from the Concatenated Order of Grizzled Old Geezers and even my grandchild-loving wife was reprising her sometime lament about making life with a guy who just doesn't know where to stop.

We were entrusted with the transport of Simone, seven. Simone lived under a raven's nest of dark curls and was as supercharged as most seven-year-olds. Well, a bit more maybe. Quite a bit more. She was impulse personified. On the first day in Mexico she almost ran in front of a chicken bus—not realizing that Mexican drivers view pedestrians somewhat the same way Dustin Byfuglien viewed the Sedins.

After one quick lesson in how to use her new snorkelling outfit, Simone set out straight for Cuba and was not a bit happy about being reined in and restricted to the two-fathom line. I spent the first night wide-eyed with visions of all the ways she might destroy herself—or

destroy Mexico—and asked myself for the ninety-ninth time what I had been thinking. I was already exhausted after one day of chasing after her yelling "No, no, no ..." which she turned into a rap duet with her cousin Sophie—

Papa say no no no
Don't go go go
We say ho ho ho

They kind of neutralized each other but you still couldn't take your eyes off them for a minute. At least I could do my lifeguarding from a beach chair as they swirled up and down the sand like a small tornado, and only occasionally had to make a flying tackle to save some bikinied sunbather from being trampled.

Coping with kids that age is only possible if you just set your own better judgment aside and devote yourself completely to viewing the world through the keyhole of seven-year-old whim. If you have to ignore the bonanza of fresh seafood in local restaurants in search of the one place that offers desiccated chicken nuggets, well just quit whining and do your duty. If your plan to show off the psychedelic fantasy world of the snorkelling reef is hijacked by a sudden preference for collecting derelict coconuts from village ditches, just get with the program, Papa. That reef isn't going to go away, but the innocent charms of childhood vanish quicker than summer dew.

This was brought home to us when the second week rolled around and the kids went home, leaving Mary and me alone with a few days that were supposed to be spent doing our own thing. The silence descended on the condo like a wet beach blanket and rather than relief we felt something closer to desolation. We did our best to suck it up and remember those fond holiday plans we had been putting aside but nothing held out much appeal. We both felt a little wobbly, and I noticed something glistening on

Mary's cheek as she studied a tiny sock retrieved from under the bed. Well, that's what grandmothers do. Grandfathers are made of sterner stuff.

Until I stepped outside and saw Simone's precious collection of brown and broken coconuts, still spilling across the walkway outside our door. It took me five trips to pack them back to the fetid ditches where she had so excitedly discovered them, and I was snuffling before I was done.

Even though we spent the last four days moping, Mary and I both agreed it was the best trip to Mexico ever.

The High Cost of Hesitation

One of the more uncomfortable neighbourhood squabbles on the Sunshine Coast involves a tug-of-war over docks between the shíshálh Nation and the good folk of Pender Harbour. Nobody quite knows how it started, but the long and the short of it is that the shíshálh have been blocking applications for new wharves in the Harbour for fifteen years, citing their Aboriginal land claim. Pender Harbour is the one of the best small-boat harbours on the coast, with some of the priciest waterfront, and halting dock development over such a long period has quickened pulses like few other issues in its history. But one possible advantage is that it is now possible to utter the words "aboriginal land claims" without having everybody yawn and sidle across the room to the discussion of mentholized kale chips. Canadians of all colours have been yawning about land claims for hundreds of years and are just now beginning to encounter the full cost of doing that.

Of course it is not just a coastal issue. Reports coming in from around BC indicate recent friction between the shíshálh and dock owners is not just coastal cussedness. It's all part of a much bigger battle stretching across the country.

But it is all rooted in that impulse to run and hide whenever talk turns to land claims, so a thirty-second review of the subject may be in order. I won't attempt to get into the larger historical, philosophical, anthropological, sociological and judicial aspects, upon which many dense tomes have been published. I will limit my focus to the dollars and cents of it only. It's only one facet of the picture, but it's quite a facet.

BC First Nations in general and the shíshálh in particular have been urging the government to settle the land claims issue for over a century and it would have been a lot simpler—and cheaper—if both parties had got down to business a long time ago.

Actually settlers in most parts of Canada did attempt to legalize occupation of their land by signing treaties with original inhabitants and didn't exactly bankrupt the treasury doing it. Under the eleven so-called "numbered treaties" signed between 1871 and 1921, many First Nations received the princely annuity of five dollars a head for each regular band member and sometimes a decent chunk of farmland for each family unit. Such is the wondrous logic of British law, these skinflint treaties still hold water.

The shíshálh first tried to get their claim recognized during the time of the numbered treaties and might have settled on similar terms but colonial administrators took the position that there was no need to give away good fivers when they could just blow smoke instead. The result of this tactic, repeated down through the ages, was that inflation kept puffing up the Sechelt payable until, by 1999, government negotiators tried to settle it for $43.5 million cash plus a thousand hectares of land, which the band refused.

Mike Harcourt was the first BC premier to get truly serious about solving land claims and I remember asking him how much the total tab would be to settle all the BC land claims that were still outstanding in 1991, when I was attempting to become one of his MLAS. Using the yardstick of settlements in Alaska, where Native Americans got $12,500 per capita plus 10 per cent of the state land mass in 1971, and the Yukon, where First Nations got $50,000 per capita plus 13 per cent of the territorial land mass in 1990, we figured it would take $10 billion cash ($50,000 x 200,000) plus a sizeable land allocation of maybe up to ten million hectares.

"We can do that!" Mike said. "And we should."

Despite Mike's good work in setting up the BC Treaty Commission, government and First Nations lawyers have continued to talk in expensive circles ever since, delivering little in the way of treaties but burning up over $1 billion in costs.

So how much would a comprehensive BC land claims settlement cost now? Judging by the price of beer, which has doubled since 1991, the ballpark figure today must be at least 2 x $10 billion = $20 billion for the cash portion—all else being equal. But all else is not equal. Over that same period the Supreme Court of Canada has rewritten the book on Aboriginal land and title rights, making them much more valuable. In 1991 they were seen as much less than private property rights held by non-Aboriginals, involving only some limited rights to hunt, fish and do drum dances. Since the June 2014 Supreme Court decision favouring the Tsilhqot'in, Aboriginal title has been redefined as superior to private ownership. It now includes exclusive use of the land as well as everything on and underneath the land. This ratchets up the value of Aboriginal title by many times, so the cost of compensation goes up many times too. Can you say $60 billion? How about 100? How much further can a BC land claims resolution be put off before the price tag is beyond the provincial treasury's ability to pay, if it isn't already? Perhaps Nisga'a leader James Gosnell's famous claim that BC First Nations own the province "lock, stock and barrel" is not so far-fetched as it once seemed. In 2015 the BC Liberal government rolled out a new "Reconciliation Commitment Document" aimed at making piecemeal settlements that would push the day of reckoning even further into the future. In 2018 the Sechelt's first instalment under the reconciliation process brought them $36 million in cash, three blocks of land and a to-be-determined amount of control over forestry and mineral resources throughout the claim area. This is just an interim payment, mind you. No information was offered as to how this would affect a final settlement, if there ever is one. The reconciliation process is open-ended.

The Tsilhqot'in decision also made it easier for First Nations to establish their title, granting it on land that is only occasionally used by members rather than limiting it to intensively used land as before. This allowed the Tsilhqot'in to secure title to 40 per cent of their historic claim area, netting them 175,000 hectares. The shíshálh claim area totals 390,000 hectares, so if the court applied the same rule there the shíshálh would get 156,000 hectares rather than the 1,000 hectares the government offered in 1999.

No one can fault shíshálh leadership for pushing its claim in light of the Tsilhqot'in breakthrough. It wouldn't be doing its job if it did otherwise. Whether or not one agrees with the newly defined legal reality is beside the point. It is now the law of the land. It would hardly be defensible for the government to say to First Nations, "Oops, turns out that British legal system we've been forcing you to live under all these centuries isn't working in our favour now, so we're chucking it." No, Canada made that bed and must lie in it. What would make a lot of sense would be to face the land claims issue head-on and settle it before it balloons up any bigger than it already has. Then, one suspects, neighbour-hood squabbles over things like dock leases would vanish in a puff of sweetgrass smoke.

The Great Undoing

At about quarter to five on the afternoon of October 18, 2015, my poor old papa, Frank White, who has supplied me a lot of good lines over the years, finally made it over his last hill, hauled his last load of logs, cracked his last one-liner, said his last goodbye and breathed his last breath. He was ready. He was 101.

"And a half!" I can hear him chiming in with his trademark deadpan.

I call him poor only because he had gotten so old and because at the end I think he really wanted to stick around longer but finally had to call it quits. That was one of his lines, "call it quits," usually used for ending a day of work, which he seldom did until forced by darkness or exhaustion and often both. He was what some people, but not him, would call a working fool. He worked for the sake of working. He had no use for people who didn't work, even though he never greatly profited from his own work. Another irony about his work attitude is that after working flat out for seventy-odd years, he got to spend three decades sampling how the other half lives, courtesy his second marriage to the *New Yorker* author and bon vivant Edith Iglauer. With Edith he attended art openings and operas, hiked the Great Wall, rode the Trans-Siberian Railway, dined with famous celebrities and generally lived the life of Riley. But when asked to compare the two phases of his life, the first seventy years of bruising labour and the last thirty years of cultured ease, he had no hesitation in saying he preferred the working phase. Because, he said, it was more "real."

It was quite a journey. I don't mean the whole hundred-and-one-and-a-half years of it, which filled two volumes of memoirs that according to him, "didn't get the half of it." I mean his final journey, after he and his beloved fellow adventurer Edith Iglauer first started getting to the stage where they needed a little outside help, for all that they refused to admit it. Numerous well-meaning acquaintances began to suggest we should "find them some nice place" (translation: nursing home) as much as fifteen years ago, when they were still doing eleven-city tours of Europe and driving across the US twice a year. Dad responded he would eat a pound of rat poison before he'd let himself be put in a "home," to which Edith added, "Make sure you leave a pound for me."

I'm glad they were so clear about that. It saved us from one of the most agonizing decisions most families with elderly parents have to make. We were stuck keeping Dad and Edith in their own little waterfront shack whether we wanted to or not. Friends of mine whose parents are only in their seventies are already wrestling with this dilemma, but it says something about Dad and Edith's intrepidness that they didn't give us cause for concern until they were both well into their nineties. This doesn't mean we were spared the histrionics so many go through with elderly parents; it just means for us it was crammed into one brief, hair-raising spasm.

We experienced all the geriatric rites of passage, beginning with the tug-of-war over driver's licences. Both Dad and Edith were addicted to their wheels and furthermore, really needed them since they lived in a rural location with no public transit. Dad had been a great driver for the first eighty years or so, but toward the end his aim was getting pretty wide. I remember one day noticing a great fresh skive in the side of his Honda.

"Is that new?" I asked.

"What?" he said. "I don't see anything."

"This giant scrape right here. The trim has been peeled off the whole length of the car."

"Oh, that little scratch," he said. "I guess some SOB sideswiped me in the IGA parking lot and ran off." On my way out of the carport I noticed a curled-up piece of Honda door trim beside one of the roof support posts, which had been knocked crooked.

We fought the driving war for another year or so and even surreptitiously enlisted the help of the Superintendent of Motor Vehicles—who took Dad's side. But as with so many elder care issues, passing time provided the cure. Once the Oldtimer Express starts on that final downward pitch, the riders' own inner clocks start accelerating. It's like early childhood, except in reverse. In his book Dad called it The Great Undoing. Eventually he gave up his keys voluntarily.

"I'm too scared to ride with myself anymore," he said.

The same with help in the home. When we first proposed getting one of those nice live-in caregivers, the idea of sharing their home with "some stranger" made them recoil in horror. A few years later, they were calling Digna their guardian angel and making her promise to never leave.

I could write a book about the wonderful world of walkers, handholds, bathtub lifts, handicapped eating utensils, lift chairs, Ultra Overnight Depends, motorized wheelchairs, Temporary Foreign Worker Program regulations and much more that I became familiar with during the final five years. (*Tip:* Elder care appliances are very expensive new but are given away practically free every day on Craigslist. In fact I still have a carport full you can have for the taking.)

Dad was sailing along like he'd go on forever until Christmas 2014, when he took a nosedive. It looked like a stroke to us, but by this time the medics had one blanket diagnosis for all his ills: "Hey, he's a hundred years old!" They waited until they were pretty sure he had less than six weeks left before calling in the palliative homecare team, but he was still having too much fun flirting with nurses and holding Edith's hand at night to co-operate. Ten months later, he was still dragging the palliative care team out to Garden Bay every day. I think he blew a pretty big hole in their budget, and they were getting noticeably antsy.

"If anything serious happens," I was cautioned more than once, "don't call the ambulance. Call the undertaker."

I don't know if Dad overheard, but if he did I'm sure he would have just wheezed a quiet cackle. The only thing that was still working at the end was his sense of humour. He couldn't speak, only whisper, and in what was to be our last conversation, when I asked him how he was doing, he husked something that sounded like "just eyeballs and ... [something]."

I had to laugh.

I knew what he was trying to say. It was one of his old sayings, borrowed from the days of ox logging when some bullpuncher earned his place in history by saying his ox team was so worn out all that was left of them was "eyeballs and ..."—well, this is a family publication so let's just say you could mistake it for "ash holes."

Pop slipped away leaving us all smiling, which is just the way he would want it. It is hard to feel too bad about a guy who got so much more out of this life than most do.

Edith, bless her, kept on trucking, but then she was a mere ninety-eight. She spent most of the day snoozing in her recliner, periodically waking to ask "Where's Frank?" I just kept repeating "He's gone away." I resisted the temptation to point out he was actually in that small cardboard box in the hall closet, which I am sure would have caused his ashes to utter a muffled chuckle.

Fixed-Link Follies

I see we are into another round of fixed-link follies here on the Sunshine Coast. It seems to afflict every community dependent on ferries and periodically even drives residents of Victoria to ponder replacing the Swartz Bay–Tsawwassen run with a system of bridges, causeways and tunnels costing in the trillions—anything to free them from those four-sailing waits on long weekends.

Here on the Sunshine Coast, whenever the ferry service between Horseshoe Bay and Langdale has a particularly bad season, or a whole run of bad seasons as is the case at present, people get thinking there's got to be a better way. They get out their chart of Howe Sound and begin searching for ways to circumvent the ferry link by building roads or bridges, hoping to discover some brilliant solution missed by generations of previous seekers. Alas, Anvil Island is found to be just as far from Lions Bay, the sheer bluffs along the west side of Howe Sound just as sheer and the passes through the Tantalus Range just as impassable as ever.

Normally the fixed link is regarded as a fit topic only for on-line gossip sites or conversation lapses at the bar, but the most recent outbreak was given an unexpected gloss of respectability by the then highways minister, who for some reason awarded an authority known as R.F. Binnie & Associates $250,000 to study the matter. Perhaps the minister was hoping the Tantalus Range has been eroded by global warming or that the last earthquake shunted Anvil Island a bit closer to shore, or perhaps he imagined this would give the illusion of being sensitive to local aspirations.

I wish the minister had called me first. I could have told him everything he needed to know for the price of a coffee. You could settle the matter with no more research than a glance at the free map on the latest visitor guide.

The idea of a fixed link using bridges is simply dealt with. Whichever way you island-hop, across Bowen and Keats or across Anvil and Gambier, you would need three high-level bridges each more than a kilometre long. Bridges like that cost at least $200 million a kilometre, meaning that even if these crossings were feasible your bridge cost alone would be over $600 million. That's what the government spent rebuilding the Sea to Sky Highway all the way to Whistler, and that was only justified by the Olympics. What comparable draw does the Sunshine Coast offer that would justify a similar expenditure? The Dakota Ridge toboggan run is nice but I don't see it as an Olympic venue anytime soon.

Okay, forget bridges. They would probably shake to pieces in the first good Squamish gale anyway. Let's look for an all-land land route. The fixed-link fans are blogging all sorts of unsung wonder routes somebody's cousin discovered with their ATV, but the shortest one is still the most obvious one, along the west side of Howe Sound from Port Mellon to Squamish. That is about forty kilometres. Average highway building costs in Canada, not adjusted for the kind of sheer rock bluffs that exist along much of that shore, are $3-5 million a kilometre. That gives us a rock-bottom cost of $120 million. The real cost once all the blasting was done could be fifty times that, but let's go with the best case.

One hundred and twenty million? Really?

Who did the honourable minister think he was kidding? When was the last time Victoria spent $120 million or even a tenth of that trying to make the wrong-way voters of the Sunshine Coast happy? The minister was heard mumbling something about costs being offset by improved tourism and economic development, but that just showed how little he really knew the Sunshine Coast. We have a grand total of 12,800 occupied households here, an unnaturally high percentage of them by people with their productive years happily behind them. It's not as if the place was vibrating with economic potential, just waiting for a fixed link to burst upon the world stage. My dear old dad used to preach that the Sunshine Coast would someday be home to a hundred thousand Lower Mainland commuters whose homes would carpet the slopes of Mount Elphinstone, but he was the only local I ever met who welcomed that prospect and he has now taken his vision to the great bedroom community in the sky. If the minister thought the general populace hereabouts views economic development or tourism growth with unalloyed joy, he should have talked to the folks trying to build that fancy hotel in Gibsons, which engendered such an epic of community opposition its fate was still in doubt ten years later.

The inevitable conclusion of all fixed-link explorations is that there is one and only one practical way to improve access to the region, one that would accommodate natural growth, that all residents would welcome and that would cost but a minute fraction of a bridge or highway. I speak of convenient, dependable and affordable ferry service. Unfortunately, that is something successive governments seem dead set against.

The Arts

One of the annual milestones on the Sunshine Coast in addition to the coming of the summer people, the blooming of the red tide and the outbreak of flying ants is something called the Art Crawl, when every other driveway, it seems like, blossoms with banners proclaiming the occupants are engaged in some sort of artistic pursuit. In my lifetime, this is a late-arriving development. I can't think of the arts without thinking of all the original coast dwellers who would groan at the mention of the word. This is an affliction I carry from having grown up in a logging camp on Nelson Island where the average educational level was about grade 6 and anyone caught reading a tattered copy of Mickey Spillane was immediately decried as a pencil neck or an egghead and given a hard time for the next month. If the poor victim ventured an opinion about the best place to dig a choker hole the next day, the response would be, "Is that what it says in that there book?" Or, "Okay, Einstein, show us how it's done. Or did you get to that part in your book yet? Har har har." In our bunkhouse even *True* and *Argosy*, with their articles on UFO invasions and homicidal commie femmes fatales, were considered too scholarly for real loggers, although *Taboo's* all-pin-up approach enjoyed more acceptance.

When I see populists like Viktor Orbán and Donald Trump rising in the polls I think of my old bunkhouse buddies and I get it. They felt beset in a world that honoured teachers and artists, favoured big words and always seemed to be frustrating them with scissorbill excuses and rules they couldn't understand. When guys like that see someone in public life talking like Mike Hammer and making the world seem simple again, they can't resist, even if they know the man has made billions exploiting gullible fools. This is why demagoguery works. I always wonder why the more progressive parties can't conjure up a good tub-thumping demagogue. Bernie Sanders was a step in that direction, but ultimately he may have been too cerebral to gather in the blue-collar voters who should have been voting for public health care and a living minimum wage if only they had a candidate who spoke their language. I'm scratching my brain here to think of an example of a good one anywhere in the world. It's funny, that. Why should the only effective demagogues be on the far right, persuading poor people to vote against their own interests?

Part of the problem might be that this cultural hostility cuts both ways. It's not just the white male high school dropouts who carry a grudge around for those on the other side of the diploma line; the prejudice is just as strong and just as blind coming the other way. I think of some of the rancid comments heard on the grounds of the Sechelt Writers Festival in the days when the Sleepy Hollow Show 'n' Shine was being held on the same day and the revving of hemis somewhat interfered with the dulcet tones of declaiming poets. "Mouth-breathing gearheads" would be one of the politer epithets going around the Rockwood pavilion. How many times do you hear the term "beer-guzzling hockey fan" being used to designate the supposed unthinking rabble who hold Canada back from its destiny as a world leader in all things fine and cultured? I have used it myself, though I know I probably couldn't hold my own in a political argument with Tampa Bay centreman Alex Killorn, who is just one of over a hundred pro hockey players with degrees from Harvard.

I recently worked on a book with anthropologist Wade Davis, who makes a plea for recognizing all kinds of seemingly bizarre and backward voodoo and snake-worshipping tribes as being actually "no less intelligent or rational than citizens of supposedly advanced nations." If that is true, and I am sure it is, well, how about our own automobile worshippers and eight-card bingo players? Is this all-accepting outlook reserved only for the kind of societies we used to call primitive (not sure what the updated term is) or does it also apply to parts of our own society that haven't formally been given a place of honour in the cultural conversation? Culture, according to anthropologists, is simply a given people's way of life. If that is true, and I'm sure it is, then chainsaw sculpture and body art are surely as expressive of our culture as abstract painting and surrealist poetry.

When I think of those bunkhouse denizens from my boyhood, I think of the things that really defined their way of life. They had no use for a guy who couldn't run along a slippery log carrying a twisty chunk of heavy steel cable known as a choker. They took great pride in axework. The snipe on a donkey sleigh not only had to have just the right angle to slide through the muck, it had to be chopped as smooth as a baby's bum. Likewise hammering. A real logger had to be able to hold a railroad spike in place while his buddy lifted a six-pound sledgehammer over his head and drove it square on. If anybody flinched it meant squished fingers and something even more painful—loss of status. These were their arts, and they were as serious about perfecting them as any portrait painter mixing flesh tones.

One young chokerman at our camp had a good eye for sketching fishboats and, as I recall, covered the outhouse wall with them. He went on to become one of BC's best-known boatbuilders and recently managed to overcome his grade 6 education enough to write a bestselling book about his experiences. He has been charming audiences of loggers, fishermen and book lovers up and down the coastal reading circuit ever since. It's a good reminder that in the right hands the arts can be a force for breaking down the walls that separate us.

The Great Canadian Biffy

If you must have a proctologist, I guess it's good to have one with a sense of humour. On a recent maintenance call I noticed mine had themed his waiting room with a collection of books bearing such titles as *Outhouses of the West, Outhouses of the East, Outhouses of Alaska, The Nova Scotia Outhouse Reader, Ode to the Outhouse, Outhouses I Have Known, Flushing Out America's Hidden Treasures, Outhouse to Penthouse, Outhouse in the Outback, An Otter in the Outhouse, There's a Porcupine in My Outhouse, Uncle John's The Haunted Outhouse, Morry Moose's Time-Traveling Outhouse Adventure!* and *Crash Landing into a Field of Outhouses.* Whatever it is that captivates people about biffies, I am a confirmed subscriber to it. Every time I visit Dr. Chuckles he has added a few more titles and I always find myself flipping through them in rapt fascination.

Sadly we have so far been denied a *Great Privies of the Sunshine Coast*, but after exploring an old homestead in Desolation Sound, Gibsons poet Peter Trower once wrote a moving elegy called "Outhouse":

> *A few more snows and winds will flatten ...*
> *Those fragile skull-eyed shacks ...*
> *But not the outhouse ...*
> *Built for the wars, that crapper*

Fashioned solid and lovingly
With even scrollwork around the eaves
Straddled on two skookum logs
Over the narrow creek mouth.
Self-flushing—
An ingenious joy of a john.
To sit with ruminative pipe
On bird-rustling evenings
It must have been his favourite place
Planning a confident kingdom
To last at least forever

As a kid I spent some of my most satisfying moments in outhouses and I miss them. Yeah, I know readers think I am indulging in foolish sentimentality and could not possibly mean I would trade in my tiled, heated, ventilated, American Standard lo-flush, and they're right. But it is not only old fossils like myself who fall prey to the charms of the earth closet.

For the past several years I have been involved in restoring the Ameliasburgh, Ontario homestead of Canada's celebrated national poet Al Purdy, and at one point we took a class of local high school students down for a tour. The thing that caught their attention was not the writing room where Purdy delivered himself of such immortal lines as "Keep your ass out of my beer!" but his sagging, weedy old outhouse. They had apparently never seen one before and were fascinated by this ancient technology for capturing the by-products of genius. They were so taken with it that by the end of the tour they had persuaded their teacher to let them truck it back to shop class and restore it to its former glory as host to some of our nation's most inspired posteriors. They worked on it for a year and the story of the Trenton kids taking whole afternoons away from playing Pokémon Go to rebuild a 1950s comfort station went viral, generating more cheerful press than our entire effort to restore the Purdy estate.

I can hear my late, sainted mother grumbling, "Easy to get all romantic about outhouses when you never had to use one in pouring rain in the middle of the night." And Mother is right as usual. A lot of the nostalgia for outhouses is really nostalgia for the era when they were used, a simpler time when all men talked like Donald Trump. But I think there is still something to be said for the innate qualities of outhouses themselves.

Most people assume pit toilets were very bad for the environment, but this is not necessarily so. Once I was fishing on Homesite Creek and I stopped to dig worms at an abandoned homestead much like the one Trower described. The ground was rocky and I was having a hard time scratching a hole anywhere until I saw this nice soft-looking grassy patch. I jammed my digging stick into it and it sunk in about a foot. I began turning over sods and excavating fluffy, black, sweet-smelling loam laced with fat, lively angle worms I could tell were just dying to go swimming. I plunged my hands in and began fingering them into an old tobacco can, rejoicing in my good fortune, until I unearthed some telltale items that made it clear I was elbow-deep in a former privy pit. I couldn't quite bring myself to use those worms to hook trout intended for the family table, though I knew I was probably being overly fastidious. After all, whatever this excessively fecund organic material had started out as, there was no doubt natural processes had long since transformed it into the finest-quality humus. I am not sure modern municipal sewage disposal strategies have a more benign outcome.

Outdoor biffies had their deplorable side, as any pioneer mother would be quick to point out. There was that long hike in all degrees of desperation and freezing weather, although the cold season had the advantage of mitigating the facility's fragrance, which no amount of lime and cross-ventilation could prevent from becoming overpowering in times of heat. And no matter how much you tried, it was impossible to avoid occasionally sneaking a peek down the hole and witnessing undeniable proof that the most pretentious members of the community were still just manure-producing beasts at bottom. People who grew up using outdoor loos learned not to take themselves or anybody else too seriously. I think that had a good effect on society generally, something we could do with a little more of in these punctilious times.

Of Grizzlies, Oilers, Pigs and Wacey Rabbit

When a Sunshine Coast native named Peter Toigo Jr. had the audacity to start a WHL hockey team in Vancouver under the very noses of the NHL Canucks a few years ago, I and many other fans gave a cheer. Like big-league sports teams everywhere, the Canucks sucked BC taxpayers in for millions of dollars in tax breaks, free infrastructure and outright grants on the basis they were supposed to rally regional morale and provide good advertising for Vancouver. They rewarded our support by setting a world record for wretched performance by a sports team, thereby establishing the name Vancouver in the minds of people everywhere as a synonym for "hopeless loser," an impression only mildly relieved in the 2010s by a blip of above-average play, now a fading memory. As for boosting morale, the Canucks' Guinness record in futility only deepened British Columbians' natural tendency to believe that they are somehow condemned to dwell on the hinder end of civilization. Add to this the fact that the greedy sots who own the Canucks charge as much to watch their team flounder as it would cost for a weekend getaway to Loss Vegas, and you can see why a lot of us rejoiced at the news that Pete Toigo, who served his tycoon apprenticeship in his mom-and-pop store in Powell River, was starting a new Vancouver hockey team of eager youngsters that you could see for the price of a six-pack. When poor attendance forced this brave team to relocate to Langley I had to admit I had never once gone to see them despite the fact they won a Memorial Cup and better, boasted a centre whose true name (google it if you don't believe me) was Wacey Rabbit.

I blame the team name.

They were called the Giants.

Giants? As in New York football or San Francisco baseball? Why couldn't they have found a name with some local resonance, like Salmonbellies? A few years after Vancouver, Chilliwack jumped into the game with their own WHL team. Its name? Bruins. That might have made some sense if they'd been an affiliate of the Boston Bruins, but they weren't. No wonder the team was sent packing after a few seasons. In the Chilliwack of today, the word *bruin* is not associated with strength and ferocity, but with eating garbage. There was an unfortunate parallel here with the kind of hockey the team played. You'd think the team's PR people would have spent a few minutes asking themselves what Chilliwackers think about when they think good thoughts about themselves (Milkers? Manure Spreaders?) and tried to link their team to that.

What is it with sports owners that their roster of proper nouns is shorter than Donald Trump's attention span? Names like Lions, Tigers, Bears, Giants, Royals and Kings are as threadbare as Ryan Getzlaf's pate. Memphis Grizzlies? How long has it been since an actual grizzly bear was seen in Memphis? This fierce predator was extirpated from Tennessee in the late nineteenth century, along with the buffalo and the passenger pigeon. Same with panthers in Florida. No wonder these teams have such sad histories—they are named after environmental disasters.

Oilers is a name to give pause. Recycled from a failed Texas football team, it is in a way appropriate for a hockey team representing Canada's petro-province, but did none of Peter Puck's high-priced marketing consultants ever bother to look up what the term *oiler* really means? In the real world an oiler is a guy in greasy coveralls, usually a green kid or a burnt-out oldster, who hangs around large machinery with an oil can administering squirts of lubricant and gofering for the alpha types who actually run the machine. I worked as oiler on a grade shovel one summer and it was the most dismal job I ever had. Edmonton has spent several decades trying to crawl out of the bilge of the NHL by pigging out on top draft picks—players who would be can't-miss stars on any other team, but who step off the plane in Edmonton and immediately turn into, well, oilers. Before spoiling any more good young talent, Edmonton should do something about that name. God knows, the oil patch has lots to choose from. "Roughnecks" and "Wildcats" have been snapped up but "Toolpushers" is still available.

Professional sports teams could learn something from studying the nomenclatural history of teams here on the Sunshine Coast. When I was twelve I played on a Little League team called the Tyees, certainly a handsome handle for proud representatives of a fishing village. We couldn't hit a pitched ball, but nobody could touch us at jigging herring. Pender Harbour also has a men's soccer team called the Bananas, which is something like the Salmonbellies: I'm not sure how it fits but it sticks with you. For my money the championship in the local naming stakes goes to the long-slogging Gibsons rugby team known as The Pigs. Given the state of playing fields on this rainy coast, that name just grunts authenticity.

Luddite's Lament

All right, I admit it, I am that guy you've all been hearing about whose VCR (or PVR or whatever it is now) blinks 12:00, 12:00, 12:00 all the time. It's true I don't know how to reset it to the right time and I deserve some of the ridicule I receive over that, but in my defence, I never asked for a clock in that particularly unuseful place. I have a perfectly good clock on the wall above it that runs on a triple-A battery and has hands. If the CBC national time signal comes on and reveals it's lost a couple minutes, I just lift the glass, tap the minute hand with an extended index finger, and presto, we're back in perfect sync with GMT. Why should I spend half an hour looking for the instruction manual for that stupid DVR or whatever and another frustrating half an hour trying to figure out why the menu shown in the book bears no resemblance to the actual TVR or whatever before chucking the thing back in the drawer (again) when I don't even *want* my HDR or whatever to bleat out the time, I just want it to shut up and record *HNIC* while I'm out fixing my stepmother's oil range. Her oil range has no digital clock. It has a warming oven instead. I am always called when that stove goes on the fritz because we are both from the 1940s and we understand each other.

I am willing to move over and give this modern technology a chance. I am very open-minded that way. But I do have a question that I think is quite reasonable. Namely, why do these propeller-heads want to improve our lives in so many ways we never asked them to? The redundant clocks on the recording thingy and the microwave and the wall oven and the telephone and the coffee maker and the electric can opener are not the only examples.

The writing program I am using to write this diatribe is constantly trying to help me by putting boxes around my paragraphs, bulletizing my sentences and changing my quotation marks to Ès, and I have to wait until our friendly nerd gets up at noon before I can get it to stop.

Someone at BC Ferries has even decided we are no longer to be trusted with the highly demanding task of flushing a toilet. The good old hand-operated lever has been replaced with an electric eye backed by a sophisticated computer program that attempts to analyze the user's movements in such a way as to provide an automated flush at the just-right moment. I guess my toileting procedure must be out of sync with the Canadian norm because I seem to trigger the flush response three or four times in the course of a single sitting. If it's on-board water they are trying to conserve, they missed the boat in my case. Then when I am finally ready for some meaningful disposal, nothing I do will induce the thing to act. I bounce up and down on the seat and pantomime what I imagine to be more normal in-cubicle behaviour, but the algorithm refuses to be triggered. Finally I have to leave the problem to the next user, hiding my face with my hat as I pass down the lineup.

Some of this unsought assistance can be downright dangerous, like these bots that try to guess which ads you might like to view based on web searches you've been doing lately. A friend of mine lately found himself having to think fast when his wife demanded to know why their internet feed was jammed with ads for websites with titles like "Wrinkled but Still Horny."

If the nerdosphere is so clever, and so determined to improve our lives, why doesn't it come up with something we really need?

For instance, The Cable Disappearer. The under of my desk is so choked with knotted cords it looks like one of those mating orgies garter snakes occasionally indulge in. Or how about an idiot light on your Visa card like the one on your gas gauge that would come on when your credit is in the danger zone? Or an app for older guys so you point your phone at that partygoer who has been greeting you warmly but you can't remember if you ever met before, with a readout that would say in large print: "Name: Cedric Snitch. Relationship to you: nephew."

I suppose that's too much to ask, but here's a definitely doable idea for one of those wannabe tech billionaires, free for the taking: a brand, let's call it Crabapple, that produces video recorders that just record, phones that just make phone calls and a whole line of devices that do exactly what you want them to. But nothing else.

Raised in Pender Harbour

Some months ago some very nice people from the local Pender Harbour library called to say they wanted to hold a garden party for my wife Mary and me because of all the books we published. We were very pleased. Over the years our scribbling habit has attracted notice in places like Ottawa, Victoria, Vancouver and Tata Lake, BC, but in forty years this was the first glimmer of organized recognition from our hometown.

I don't blame local folks for wanting to wait and see just a bit. Your old-time Penderite is naturally skeptical and they have seen a lot of fancy schemes turn out to be no more than a flash in the pan. Harbourites also have a natural modesty that leads them to think nothing can be too big of a deal if it's happening there.

In the end the garden party was cancelled because of rain and I was secretly relieved because I had been lying awake at nights worrying about how to comport myself. I was, after all, raised in Pender Harbour. In my day there were a lot of parties but not many gardens, and the only times they crossed purposes was when someone fell through a window and was lucky enough to land in the flower bed. I'm not sure Pender owned a garden big enough for a party during my formative years. The only lawn in town was in front of the BC Forest Service ranger station—since converted into a kind of hand-me-down community centre housing the library—but us kids knew better than to set foot on official government grass lest Assistant Ranger Bill Brown give us a kick in the pants—which was legal then.

We were casual enough about trespassing on old Colonel Johnstone's place next door, however, which we cut through any time we had reason to go up the trail to the Pink Palace, a.k.a. the Rigger's Roost, a.k.a. the Pender Harbour Hotel, where on a good day you could see grown-ups talking funny, falling down steps, kissing the wrong mums and other good stuff to talk about at school. The old colonel didn't like us using his property for a shortcut but he was a WW I vet with a gammy leg and about all he could do was shout at us in his plummy British accent and threaten to report us to our parents, but we knew he had no idea who our parents were.

The people on the other side of the ranger station, the Larsons, were another matter. An illegal kid trail ran across Larson's Resort to the realm of the Duncans and Gooldrups who had cute daughters our age and, more important, mums who were generous with Freshie and Oreos. To visit them legally you had to hike up a towering mountain road opposite where the fire hall is now, whereas a breakneck dash across Larson's auto court would get you into Oreo territory in half the time on level ground. The Larsons were just as determined to keep scruffy bushrats from cutting across their property as Colonel Johnstone, but they were much better at it. Both were very spry and Mr. Larson would do things like hide behind trees and leap out at you, grabbing you by the britches and dragging you back to the ranger station side by your ear, where you would be dispatched with a kick in the pants and a warning your name was being sent to the police. This made a crossing of the Larson's Resort property truly terrifying, and thus much more tempting.

Mr. Larson was the prime local villain in our childish world and nobody got more of our attention on Halloween, the day set aside, as we understood it, for Pender boys to get back at all the grown-ups who'd been unpleasant to them during the year. The Larsons knew what they were in for and spent every Halloween nervously patrolling their property late into the night, shouting threats and warnings about what they'd do if they got their hands on one of us snot-nosed little delinquents. I often wondered if they had an inkling what rich adventure they were providing us and how much easier their lives would have been had they just invested in some Freshie and Oreos.

V.

Scientifically Enlarging the Facts

Searching for a Coastal Icon

Lately there's been quite a patriotic dust-up about who has the world's biggest fake moose, Moose Jaw, Saskatchewan, or Stor-Elvdal, Norway. It has been a cruel blow to Canadian pride to find that *Storelgen*, Norway's elegant stainless-steel roadside attraction, is a few millimetres taller, not to mention a whole lot classier, than Moose Jaw's crumbling concrete Big Mac. The whole brouhaha is enough to make one grateful to be living in a place that doesn't feel the need to caricature some key aspect of local identity in the form of an oversized roadside geegaw. At the same time, I can't resist trying to picture just what sort of supersized icon one would choose if one were to enlist the Sunshine Coast in this international urinating contest. Sudbury has its Big Nickel, Wawa has its Great Goose—what could we put up?

We do have iconic old Molly's Reach—a liquor store before it became a world-renowned sitcom set—hovering over Gibsons' frantic five-way intersection, causing summer traffic jams, but in honesty it must be admitted that whole *Beachcombers* thing was kind of an ersatz view of coast life imposed by outsiders rather than anything of truly local origin.

We have some nice iconic totem poles thrusting up in front of various Sechelt Nation properties, but they hardly set us apart from places like Duncan, which has already claimed the title "City of Totems." That's funny because neither Sechelt nor Duncan was noted for totem poles back in the day. The original Coast Salish carvers tended to create massive human figures balanced on towering legs rather than the familiar poles consisting of stacked-up crests, which was more of a north coast thing. One of those big old wooden bodies would be distinctive looming alongside Highway 101 on its log legs, but that's not the style these days.

So what else, a totemic beast? This isn't really grizzly country and black bears have a bit of an image problem. Salmon were big here but we couldn't pretend to compete with the 120-pound tyees of Rivers Inlet. We did get an early start on the killer whale reconciliation project what with the famous whale-hunting exploits at Pender Harbour in 1968 and '69, but Corky and Hyak long since went Hollywood, taking their iconic value with them. So much for the animal kingdom; what about vegetables?

Actually, there we may have something. In the early days of settlement the Sunshine Coast had some of the most impressive vegetation this side of Redwood Country. Sure, in those days the whole south coast was forested with sky-scraping Douglas fir, but ours were arguably as big as anyone's. The massive logs used to build Lumberman's Arch in Stanley Park were cut by the Klein clan in their backyard up at Kleindale, and trees towering over three hundred feet in height and over twelve feet in girth were not uncommon. By the early twentieth century the Sechelt Peninsula was criss-crossed with railroads used to haul the tall timber to tidewater, often carrying one huge log per car. One of those behemoths would be a real traffic stopper alongside our section of the Pan American Highway, and would make Prince George's vaunted spruce mascot, Mr. PG, look like a piece of kindling. The problem would be to find a working example. There are only a handful of true old-growth fir left standing and they tend to be in protected reserves like the Big Tree Park in West Sechelt. Removing one would not be popular, even for the greater glory of the Sunshine Coast tourist industry.

What we do have in abundance however, are the stumps of those great gone goliaths, charismatic monuments that stud coastal undergrowth from Egmont to Port Mellon, often bearing the steps cut in them by pioneer handfallers trying to climb up to the narrower, less gnarly part of the trunk. Some are huge. Back in the fifties one at Port Mellon was hollowed out and used as a bunkhouse by the logger poet Pete Trower. Most are a little punky by now but the sturdiest could be restored with a bit of silicone, Cuprinol and steel bracing like they used to rebuild the Drive-Through Tree in Stanley Park. There could be a public search to find the likeliest example. Then it could be carefully dug out and mounted on a concrete plinth at the Langdale brake check where it could serve as a monument to the once-mighty forest industry, which some people credit with building this place and others with wrecking it. People could take from it what they wanted, which is what you want in public art.

Spring and All

Ah, spring. We west coasters don't realize it but we are somewhat deprived when it comes to the season of renewal. We experience a very understated quickening of nature's pulse from about mid-February when the snowdrops appear, closely followed by the first daffodils, until about June 15 when the more efficient home gardeners are already harvesting leaf lettuce. There are days along this even continuum when you step outside in the morning and say to yourself, "Is that the first robin? Have I noticed those maple flowers before, or was that last year? What is the source of that wonderful bracing scent? I haven't smelled that in months." Our springs are pleasant but you have to pay attention to even know they're happening.

I never knew what spring was until I spent one in Mayo, Yukon. In early April we convoyed into our placer mine on the South McQuesten (pronounced "McQuestion" by real Yukoners) when the place was still frozen hard as granite. The Yukon, that part of it anyway, gets only a smattering of snow so the road was good for driving except for the "glaciers." Glaciers in this usage are not permanent icefields high in the mountains but places where a trickle of water crossed the road and instead of threading through the cross-ditch, froze in place. As the trickling continued over the winter, it would continue to freeze and mound up until it formed an ice dome the size of the Sechelt arena. This was why the convoy

166

had a D8 Cat breaking trail, and even it had a hard time busting through some of these ice mountains.

We had to get to camp early in the season because around mid-April the first stage of the northern spring began, a phenomenon we fortunately know nothing of down here in the banana belt, something called "breakup." Breakup is when everything thaws. As the spring days lengthen, the eaves start dripping, then the thin Yukon snow disappears, then the creek starts groaning and snapping, then all hell breaks loose. Water comes rushing down the valley like a burst dam, flooding every low area, cutting off the roads and washing away anything not parked on high ground.

By this time you better have your camp set up and all supplies you're going to need for the next month, because from here on all roads are impassable gumbo and even walking from the bunkhouse to the cookhouse becomes perilous. Step in the wrong place and you're going to need two strong swampers with a rope to extract you from the bottomless muck. This is the longest and most unpleasant part of the northern spring, seeming to go on forever, though I guess it wasn't much over a month.

It seemed like the entire universe had turned to mush so completely it would never be solid again, but this was failing to account for the next unexpected feature of the northern spring—the galloping increase in the length and strength of the awakening sunshine. By the end of May there is only about four hours of nighttime left, and a lot of that is twilight. The rest is rampaging sunshine. The gumbo in the camp yard and on the roads has been getting a little stiffer each day, then suddenly it is throwing off dust.

That's when spring really begins. One day the campsite is brown and barren and then the next day it has a slight greenish cast. The next day it is solid green. Two days after that it is a carpet of three-inch-high plants showing signs of buds. Ten days later it is a sea of brilliant colour. I remember noticing a weed by my bunkhouse door one day, then watching it unfold into a luscious purple Arctic lupine that kept shooting up until it was waist-high. I was not into flowers at that time but the rampaging growth of that plant made my jaw drop. It was like watching one of those time-lapse films happening in real time.

There was a soundtrack to go with this spectacle. When we first arrived the place was as silent as a grave, except for the occasional squawking of the resident raven. By the time the lupine was ankle-high the place was alive with birdsong and the air was swarming with what our Tutchone catskinner collectively referred to as "summer birds"—too numerous to have individual names for. Swarming also with buzzing insects, which we combatted by closing our eyes, pinching our nostrils and bombing all exposed skin with full-strength Raid.

Now, that was a spring worthy of the name. I'm glad I saw it—once. It was followed by a summer barely six weeks long before frost returned in late August, then fall came on like a runaway freight train. Here on the coast we are so lucky to have seasons we can ignore.

Muse in Caulk Boots

When Aunt Jean died in 2019 at the age of one hundred, one thing she insisted on was that nothing be written about her. No notices, no articles in papers.

"I don't want a lot of people saying, 'Oh, that old bat finally packed it in—good riddance!'"

She mentioned it quite pointedly in my direction, several times, because of all the people in our family I was the most likely to be writing something in the papers. You'd think she'd have known better. Her very mention of it got me thinking about this article, wondering how I could squeeze her long and uncommon story into a few pages.

Aunt Jean and I had a bit of history when it came to stories. In fact, before she called me to her hospital bed to say good-bye, she'd been giving me the silent treatment for several years over something I'd written about her side of the family that she considered somewhat exaggerated. It got me nowhere trying to argue that if I ever gave in to the temptation to exaggerate a little bit, it was probably her fault.

Jean was my mum's younger sister. They both grew up on dairy farms in the Fraser Valley under the lash of a hardbitten Hebridean mother who viewed children as God's gift of free labour. According to my dad, who was anything but objective on the subject of his in-laws, my mum was generally chained to the kitchen stove while Jean's special area of indentured toil was the barn. They were both quite beautiful as young women but Jean's charms were usually hidden under mannish garb redolent of the barnyard.

Jean always objected when Dad referred to the Boley farm as a child labour camp and defended her old oppressor in a most undeserved way but the record shows that at the earliest chance she fled the farm for work that paid. One of her first jobs was building Canso flying boats at a wartime assembly plant on Lulu Island. She also did a Rosie-the-Riveter turn in the wartime shipyards. Perhaps because of her early experience shovelling out barns, she readily took to what would now be called non-traditional work and when I first got to know her she was working in my dad's logging camp as a whistlepunk, wearing caulk boots and hardhat and giving as good as she got on a crew of unenlightened 1950s bush apes who believed it was a slight upon their manhood to be forced to work alongside a woman.

Jean inherited an ample measure of her mother's Highland cantankerosity and after a spectacular set-to with my dad, departed the Green Bay camp taking with her the camp's key piece of equipment, a yarding donkey, and Dad's erstwhile business partner, Charlie. They ran their own show up Jervis Inlet for a few years before Jean went solo as a camp cook, travelling

the length and breadth of the coast whupping up grub for lusty loggers with one hand while beating off their advances with the other. Not that it bothered her. Any guy who tried to get smart with her had better be prepared for a withering put-down, if not a hot skillet between the eyes. I knew a lot of women like her in the old days. Sexism? They figured they knew what men were made of and preferred to have it out in the open where they could stomp on it. They were more uncomfortable with smoothies who came on as gentlemen, or heaven forbid, "feminists," viewing them as unnatural sneaks. But much as she felt at home in it, in time even Jean grew weary of beating her way around the camp cookhouse circuit. Sometime in the 1980s she plunked some of her savings down on a nice house in Roberts Creek and as a way of easing into retirement, launched a new career in homecare.

As kids we enjoyed Aunt Jean because she was such a bad influence. One Halloween she talked us into making a realistic dummy with some of Dad's old work clothes and placing it in the middle of Francis Peninsula Road. Several cars swerved around it without slowing, but when the town's leading citizen came along with his station wagon full of churchgoers they responsibly rolled to a stop several yards short of the apparent casualty and engaged in an anxious debate about what to do. Finally Mr. Murdoch hesitantly got out and tiptoed up to the dummy, before erupting in outraged shouts.

"You goddamned kids! I know who you are and your parents will hear about this!" he roared, addressing the bushes opposite where we were hiding. Terrified, we ran to Aunt Jean for protection but she just laughed.

"You say they were waving their arms and arguing? I bet he was wetting his pants, the old fraud! I can't wait to spread this one around the Legion!"

It was Jean who taught me the benefits of occasionally stretching the truth a little bit. Not fibbing exactly, but scientifically enlarging facts by shifting them along in the direction they want to go anyway. In the 1950s the truth was pretty humdrum and badly needed some improving. In Jean's storytelling, ordinary happenings became laughable farces. Everybody's nose was bigger, their walk more staggery, their talk slangier, their deeds goofier. And I couldn't help noticing how much more entertaining that made our normally uninspiring everyday reality. When I started copying her style, I also noticed how much more attention I got from adults who usually ignored me, for all that they would caution me against telling tall tales once they stopped laughing.

Some readers might be tempted to draw a line between my early exposure to this interesting relative and my present occupation, and they wouldn't be entirely off base.

Rest in peace, Aunt Jean. You showed us all how a bit of imagination can brighten the dullest day.

Roaring Bullheads, Brainfarts and Baseball

The other day I published a book. Of poems. I apologize for this. It's not something I do often, in fact this was my first book of poems in twenty-six years. Given I dash poems off at the slightest provocation and own my own publishing company, I think once in twenty-six years shows admirable restraint.

Before readers start flipping pages in search of a more gripping topic, let me quickly mention this book has sex in it. All right, geezer sex may not be the biggest draw, but there's a bunch of other great stuff like sea otters, roaring bullheads, outhouses, broken stoves, baseball, decrepit wharves, street dancing, love, stumps, brainfarts, urologists, the pyramids, the moon, dementia and not shooting one's father. I think the technical term for this kind of book is "eclectic." I like that better than "dog's breakfast."

Let me try to explain how this odd assemblage came about.

When I was in my twenties and fresh out of college, it was my ambition to be a writer, so I had the bright idea of first becoming a publisher so I would always have a guaranteed outlet for my own work, which I was never too sure would fly on its own. This turned out to be a great idea in all ways except the main one, namely that of advancing my own writing. It turned out that a whole lot of other people who were more industrious and a lot more pushy than me also wanted to advance their own writing, so the publishing part of the scheme worked really well but the writing part not so much. Fifty years later I am still vainly trying to keep up to the flood of other folks' manuscripts that pour over the transom every day, while the great Canadian novel I started in 1976 remains stalled on page 32.

For a long time I satisfied myself by jotting down bright ideas I would work into my various magnum opuses when I finally got around to them. After raising a family, watching policemen and even prime ministers become ever younger-looking, publishing roughly a thousand books by other writers and filling several closets with cryptic notes about things I should write someday, I began to suspect a flaw in my writing strategy.

This was when I got the idea that instead of wasting all my bright ideas in unintelligible memos, I should shape them into poems. I had written a couple of poetry books in my youth and figured I knew how to do it. Whenever a line gets up to about three and a half inches, you do a hard return and start a new one. I noticed that whenever I did this, MS Word 2003, my all-knowing word-processing program, automatically began each new line with a capital letter, which I took as a vote of confidence.

As these occasional mental doodles mounted up, I began supplying some of them with pretentious titles and melodramatic endings and began to wonder if indeed a few of them might pass in public as actual poems. One day a writer whose own books I had been dutifully publishing for decades made the mistake of asking if I ever got around to writing anything of my own anymore, so I emailed him a couple hundred samples. He responded by saying, actually, yes, they were rather like poems, or if not, something else quite interesting in their own right. He even made a selection of ones he found more presentable and arranged them into an official-looking manuscript. I was encouraged but still dubious, so I sent the manuscript to a publisher who owed me no favours and had no reason to flatter me, expecting to be brought back to earth with a thud. They accepted it. Then they printed it. At their own expense. Then they got me invited to a prestigious literary festival, and paid my ticket all the way to Eden Mills, Ontario. Several reviews appeared, including one by an undeniably real poet named Linda Rogers, who wrote,

This is real poetry; one version of the gospel, and it is received with joy and gratitude because it is life stained with regret, as in 'News from Space':

> *the planet blurs into a smoky vagueness*
> *Like an old man's clouding memory*
> *Of a life once crisply faceted with possibility.*

Regret seems unavoidable however we spend our lives, but it can be leavened an occasional step out of the ruts we tend to dig ourselves. Especially when you get a few scattered shouts of encouragement.

Early Computers of the Sunshine Coast

A few months ago I got a very excited call from a young man at the local paper who had discovered the old steam donkey on top of the Caren Range. I gave him the basics on what steam donkeys were (used pre-ww II to winch logs out of the forest) but the thing he couldn't get over was how a magnificent machine the size and weight of a CPR locomotive could have been discarded in the bush rather than being mounted in a place of honour beside City Hall. I tried to explain how history sneaks up on people and they never suspect that the most ordinary, taken-for-granted things of their era will become the historical artifacts of the next, but I don't think I got through.

I should have used the example of computers. Just as taken-for-granted tools like donkey engines and two-man chainsaws have come to symbolize our grandparents' time, clunky-looking computers may turn out to be the signature artifact of our time. There is already a thriving network of obsolete-computer collectors with their own website at www.old-computers.com.

I am so old I can remember the Sunshine Coast before it possessed a single computer. Oh, you heard of them and you'd occasionally see pictures of IBMs every bit as big as the old steam donkey. In 1968 the Port Mellon pulp mill installed an IBM 1800 so bulky it had a building all of its own to contain its amazing 16 KB of memory (my cheap laptop has five hundred thousand times as much memory) but a computer was not something the average person ever expected to encounter in their own lives. It was around the time hippies were replaced by the yuppies that news began to leak out about something called the personal computer. Most of us found this a ludicrous notion. If you didn't personally have to run a pulp mill, whatever use would you have for a *personal* computer?

It was around the time Mount St. Helens erupted, near as I can make it, that the modern computer age first reached the Sunshine Coast. A night class was advertised by some fellow who promised to explain how computers were going to change our lives for the better. The fellow's first name was Ron and he lived on Snodgrass Road but I can't remember his last name. For reasons I don't understand to this day, my dear wife Mary decided to attend the class. Normally she left visions of the future and new-fangled gadgetry to me, although she has always been susceptible to the notion of changing our lives for the better. I tried to make my skepticism as plain as possible, but it had no effect. The next thing I knew she had backed her little Toyota up to the single-car garage that was our first office and was defiantly unloading boxes. Expensive-looking boxes.

Snodgrass Ron had sold her a personal computer. It turned out to be the first production-model Apple, the very one that started the computer revolution. It looked nothing like computers do today. It had a flat housing of beige plastic the size of a briefcase with a monitor the size of a large flashlight perched on top. It looked like something from Mattel. If I'm not mistaken it also had 16 KB of RAM. With software and doodahs it cost eight thousand dollars. (Multiply by three for the current equivalent).

Given that this was more than we had ever spent on anything up to that time, the conversation soon turned ugly. I was on the point of saying, "Either that computer goes or I do," but there was a look in Mary's eye that made me think better of it.

From the day we set it up, the little Apple never had a chance to cool down. Everything was output on a dot matrix printer whose print looked like chickadee tracks in the snow, but our customers were so awestruck by having a close encounter with an actual computer they paid their bills like never before. Feeble as it was, the little machine paid for itself in three months. Then just as my heart rate was getting back to normal Apple came out with the Apple II Plus, which had an amazing 64 KB of RAM! Since this miracle could be had for a mere $1,195 (don't forget to multiply by three), it seemed too good to pass up, and surely we would never have to buy another one in our lifetime ... Then came the Osborne, then the Kaypro, then the Atari, then the Radio Shack 80, then the Compaq, then the Mac, each justified as the last computer we'd ever have to buy. Our office now has twenty computers humming away and it seems we are replacing one every month.

It occurs to me now that original Apple of ours was the first working microcomputer in Pender Harbour, maybe on the Sechelt Peninsula. I don't know what became of it. Hopefully some impressionable young reporter will discover it in a basement someday ...

Undiscovered Miltons

George Weeks heads the list of my undiscovered Miltons. I first met him when he drifted into Pender Harbour on a rusty little ketch called the *Moonchild*. George was a boat person. Not the kind who escaped from Vietnam or Cuba, but the kind who spent much of their lives drifting up and down the BC coast on listing live-aboards looking for the perfect protected bay with free moorage and maybe a decent selection of other boat people to swap stories and bunkmates with. George grew up around Duncan, where his dad Waddy Weeks had been a hogger. A free copy of *Rhymes of a Western Logger* to the first reader who can define the term *hogger*. (OK: Hoggers were the aristocrats of the big railway camps, the men who piloted the most expensive and temperamental single piece of equipment—the purpose-built, low-geared, hill-climbing locomotives.)

Logging railroads and locomotives had pretty much disappeared by the time George reached working age, so he became a millwright, logging soul-killing days in the coast's pulp mills, acquiring a family and a mortgage and the whole disaster before rebelling and escaping by boat, where he continued to live for the rest of his days, taking on the odd job as watchman over mothballed logging camps or patrolling boundaries for the Department of Fisheries during summer salmon runs. All the while building on his store of tall tales and honing his skill at telling them.

By the time I met him, George was a spellbinder. Not only did he have a repertoire of captivating tales, he could imitate every accent from irate Chinese cook to Irish brogue to a 'Namgis chief in full rant. He could mouth sounds unmistakably identifiable as a Ford v8 sans muffler or a Jimmy Diesel running away and mime a man trying to bear-hug an unhappy two-hundred-pound halibut. He was the most entertaining stand-up and sit-down comedian I ever witnessed, bar none.

I was not alone in telling George he should capture his performances on video or write them down, but I think he was a bit insulted by the suggestion. He was content just to be good company at a dockside potluck and didn't appreciate the inference there was any higher calling. I tried sneaking a tape recorder into his galley once and ended up wishing I hadn't. He sensed it immediately and it was a while before I lived the transgression down. I tried remembering a few of his yarns and even published some in *Raincoast Chronicles*, but everyone agreed I totally missed the Weeks magic.

Well, okay, but I'm going to lay one on you anyway. This one is from a summer George spent on Fisheries patrol in Rivers Inlet back in the 1960s when that mid-coast fjord was something of a sockeye bonanza characterized by gold-rush style mayhem at peak run. Take it away, George:

"Far as getting busted up goes it's safer on a boat than most shore jobs. Safest job there is—if you don't count drowning.

"Gillnetters especially. Out on deck for a beer piss, boat leans one way, you lean the other—*kersplash*. Or reaching over the rollers to shake a log out of the web. They find your boat idling up against a bluff the next day, tow it into the float—nobody will tie up next to it.

"One year in Rivers we had three guys go over in one week.

"What happens then is, they turn up a few days later in other guys' nets. Guys'd see this lump coming up and think it was a drowned seal until it falls on deck and an arm flops out. Yeah!

Flop! [Mimics the flop, then mimics a look of horror.] Crap your drawers time, Mama!

"Two of these corpses showed up on schedule but the third one kept us guessing for a while.

"Fishermen are a spooky lot to begin with and you need to have done it to know just how eerie it gets out there in the middle of the night all by yourself, leaning over the stern wondering just what ghastly item the murk is going to puke up at you next. Everybody in the inlet was just quaking in their gumboots every time they saw something that wasn't a fish come into the light, figuring for sure they snagged this third stiff.

"Sonny Iverson said this particular night he got so bad he had to go knock back half a twenty-sixer before he could get the rest of his net in. Leaning over the stern to pull kelp out of the rudder post thinking what a fool he was to get so spooked, the whisky took his balance and—*plop!* He's in the soup, his faithful boat gliding serenely away into the night—but all he can think about is that damn stiff!

"'Now I'm in here with that son of a bitch!'

"He's afraid to paddle, thinking every time he reaches out he'll touch it, and once when he brushes a chunk he finds himself howling bloody blue murder.

"Then he hears something. A kind of faint swishing noise. He listens real careful and reaches around a little bit.

"There, right under his nose, is a moving line of corks. Some other dude is picking his net past him and all he has to do is grab on and wait to be saved. This works fine until he comes up to the other boat and finds he's all tangled up in the net and before he can say anything he's up over the rollers and crashes head-first on the deck and knocks himself silly.

"Of course the other fisherman just cuts loose swearing and cursing all the foul luck in the world—figuring it's the missing stiff he's hooked onto! Until Sonny starts coming to and moaning a bit—then the poor guy runs howling the whole length of the boat cursing God and praying to be saved at the same time.

"It takes Sonny fifteen minutes to calm him down enough to go get his boat."

George had just turned eighty when I got word he'd quietly slipped moorings for that perfect tie-up in the heavens, leaving nothing to mark the passing of one of the coast's most notable undiscovered Miltons. This poor sample will have to do.

Halloween People

On Halloween day, 2017, I received a special treat in the form of a new grandson, Ian Isaac White, whose clever mum Instagrammed photos of tiny I.I. dressed in a onesie with a skeleton design on it. Scary it was not. But I got thinking, this little devil will have his birthday on the same day as John Daly and Gwyn Gray Hill. That set off a firecracker of a connection for me, but for those not steeped in the lore of the old coast I guess I better try to explain.

John Daly and Gwyn Gray Hill were two legendary figures on the coast from the 1930s to the 1980s who both celebrated their birthday on October 31. John is well remembered thanks to the wonderful book *Fishing with John* by Edith Iglauer, his second wife. As a kid I enjoyed many a Halloween/double birthday at the Daly estate in Garden Bay where there was always a big bonfire and lots of Mr. Daly's weird friends from near and far. Nobody dressed in costume because there was no need. One old fisherman had a real eye patch. Another had a wooden leg on which he would strike matches to light his pipe. Sammy Lamont would be dressed only in trousers held up by Police suspenders, his Sasquatch-furred torso bared even in October rain. Daly favoured a Lenin look and spouted Mao. Pixie, the aging bombshell, would be flirting with everything in pants and the volume would be rising as the Scotch poured forth.

Even in this distinguished company, Gwyn Gray Hill, a.k.a. Grayhill, a.k.a. Old Roast, a.k.a. J.I. Rost, stood out. Gnome-like and disreputable in his kerosene-scented, twine-belted Sally Ann suit, he would have been a ringer for Charlie Chaplin's Little Tramp, except in place of lovable pathos he projected diabolical mischief. He lived on a boat and spent his days drifting from wharf to wharf up and down the BC and Alaska coasts, savouring the extravagant seascapes, collecting sensational lore and spreading scandalous gossip. He cruised the Alaska coast thirty times, reaching as far north as stormbound Cape St. Elias in his tiny ketch. He began his amazing odyssey in the 1930s and kept at it for half a century. I will not call him, as many did, "the last of the remittance men," because he rejected that label so vehemently I fear he would find a way to reach out from the grave and blight my heirs with an ancient curse. Suffice it to say he was the exiled scion of a wealthy English clan and lived off income from a family trust.

Grayhill was great company for kids because he could recite the Lord's Prayer backwards and speak pig Latin at warp speed. He had a cane that fired real bullets. He had a strange ring with an oversized diamond of lurid provenance. He revelled in mysteries, like that of the lighthouse keeper who was discovered on the beach sans head, the dungeon complete with leg irons he claimed to have discovered in a secret chamber beneath the old Brooks house in Halfmoon Bay, the lake up Loughborough Inlet filled with perfectly spherical balls composed of twigs. He had Trumpish nicknames for everybody: Edith Iglauer, who wrote about the Arctic, was "Mrs. Igloo"; Dane and Helen Campbell, who farmed wild boars, were "the PigWigglingtons"; bumptious Garth Dougan was "Mumblefrumpkin," etc.

In adult company his stock-in-trade was shock. When a hostess complained his boots were marking the carpet, he cheerfully removed them and made worse marks with his fetid, soot-soaked socks. When an upscale restaurant proved too stuffy for his liking, he jumped on a chair and began yelling, "Rat! Rat!" When the Royal Victoria Yacht Club objected to his decrepit live-abord docking too near he purchased the club's pristine flagship, the *Cherie*, spread its snowy sails out on the club dock and "waterproofed" them by brooming black crankcase oil all over them.

Many breathed a sigh of relief when Grayhill finally expired in 1987. He wasn't everybody's cup of tea, especially when served in an unwashed shaving mug, but he had been making the rounds of the coast's landlocked hamlets and homesteads and collecting our lore for so long he attained the status of a kind of regional mascot, equally shunned and loved. Knowing he and my new grandson are born under the same sign could mean wee Ian's parents are in for an interesting time.

Waste Wars

The Sunshine Coast is such a pretty place you would think the political battles would be all about trying to preserve its natural attributes. Friction of this kind does break out from time to time, but it does not supply fuel for the real epic confrontations. No, the battles that outrun any other tend to revolve around the noble topic of waste disposal. Gibsons and Sechelt have their curbside pickup and smelly-sewage-plant sagas, but the longest-running saga of all concerned the intention of regional government to close the Pender Harbour garbage dump, and the resistance of Pender Harbour people to this brave initiative.

It has often been remarked that of all the things they have to preserve in that rare beauty spot, it is odd that the one Penderites would fight hardest for is their lowly garbage dump. In the Harbour this was matched by wonderment that of all the desirable things Penderites have, it is strange that the one thing their regional neighbours should devote their most tireless efforts to taking away was their lowly garbage dump. Recent headlines about the dwindling lifespan of the coast's remaining dump at Sechelt take me back to my youth and my first encounter with this oddly durable issue.

The regional board in those visionary days saw itself in a civilizing role with respect to Pender Harbour, somewhat like the missionaries who convinced the original Harbour residents to give up potlatching and physically relocate to Bishop Durieu's boot camp in Sechelt. Whereas the missionaries believed that the first Harbourites could only be saved by Christianization, these pioneering politicos preached the gospel of Centralization. To them it was simply obvious that whatever issue came up, the only thinkable approach was to Centralize it someplace within easy driving distance of their lunchroom, which at that time was above the second-hand store in Davis Bay.

Back in Pender Harbour meanwhile, this well-intentioned drive to centralize was seen as an imperialist agenda to reduce the community to a state of colonial dependency by usurping all their key social institutions and then overtaxing them for the privilege. The dump in those days was uncontrolled and the community's favourite guilty pleasure was to spend an afternoon there watching bears, kibitzing with neighbours and looking for good stuff.

When the District announced that the Pender dump would have to be closed so garbage dumping could be centralized at Sechelt, Penderites mounted to the barricades as if their very lifeblood had been threatened. Even in those innocent times Harbourites sensed that it would not be quite acceptable to admit the dump was their most popular community institution so their spokesman formulated the issue as one of principle, a kind of political line in the sand. As he summed it up, "If we can't even hang onto our dump, nothing we have is safe."

Faced with this unexpected opposition, the District offered to replace the actual dump with a sort of simulated dump called a transfer station, which would mimic the role of a real dump so exactly that Harbourites would not even notice the difference. The only difference would be that instead of burying the garbage where it was made, it would be loaded onto trucks, hauled down Highway 101, trundled through pristine downtown Sechelt and buried fifty kilometres from where it was made. This would be done to save money. This proposal drew much derisive hooting when first revealed, but the Works Superintendent produced a bewildering array of charts and tables proving beyond any doubt that indeed the long-distance trucking option would be cheaper. Try as they might, Harbourites could not find any flaw in his calculations. It came to a head at a meeting in the board offices, which was packed with gloomy-looking Harbourites.

I was attempting to run a newspaper in the Harbour at this time but my journalism was self-taught and I didn't know the part about remaining above the fray. I had noticed that the factor that made the Pender dump so expensive to keep open was the maintenance, which was being done by a man named Dick Derby from Gibsons. Twice a week Dick had to low-bed his trackloader up from Gibsons to Garden Bay, a distance of seventy kilometres, and he was billing a huge amount for this. At a critical point in the meeting I questioned the superintendent about this apparent waste of money but he said it was necessary because there were no contractors in the Harbour area to do the work.

"Yes, there is," I said.

"Who?" he said.

"Me," I said. He laughed.

"What equipment do you have?"

This was a bit of a problem, since the only equipment I actually owned at that moment was a typewriter. But I knew somebody who had an HD5 trackloader they might loan me, so I mentioned that.

"And what would your rate be for this trackloader?" he said.

"Half what you're paying Dick," I said.

"We will have to consider that," he said. With angry Harbourites blocking every exit there wasn't much else he could say.

That is how my literary career took a slight detour and I became Supervisor of Solid Waste at the Pender Landfill. I kept the job for five years and enjoyed every minute of it.

Over the years the Pender dump controversy reared its head again and again until finally in 2009 the Regional District got up the nerve to just simply ram the change through despite opposition from some 850 petitioners representing over 80 per cent of Pender residents. This was still being justified in the name of saving money, but sealing up the old dump cost around $1 million, which alone would have covered the cost of keeping it open for many more years. The cost of operating the new transfer station (which needed more staff than a mere land-fill) and freighting tonnes of waste to Sechelt quite predictably dwarfed the costs the regional administrators claimed they had to reduce. Not only that, the increased tonnage pouring into the coast's last overtaxed landfill at Sechelt greatly shortened its life, raising the prospect of astronomical new costs to replace it. By the time all this became clear the authors of the disaster had all taken their talents elsewhere, so there was nobody to yell at. Sometimes democracy is so frustrating you wonder how we survive at all.

Water, Water

I think it's safe to say that during the run of hundred-year droughts, in recent summers Sunshine Coasters were reacquainted with the importance of our most underappreciated resource, water. Folks were re-plumbing their waterfront estates to collect bathwater for reuse in the garden and feeling very pioneery. None that I heard of actually had to miss regular showers, however.

It's lucky they are living here in the 2020s and not in the 1950s. When my family moved to Pender Harbour in 1955, most parts of the coast survived on backyard wells. Most were hand-dug surface wells, gouged into the substrate to a depth of ten feet or so.

The place my parents first rented at Canoe Pass had what we were told was a good well, a mouldy black cavern inside a dank little pumphouse so full of snakes and spiders it gave us the creeps to enter into it. The ancient Fairbanks Morse pump was paralyzed with rust and the iron piping that fed the wobbly little water tower had split during some past freeze-up so we supplied all household needs by bucket. About mid-July the well went dry and we discovered the bottom was comprised of a mini La Brea Tar Pit featuring carcasses of numerous snakes, rats and other local wildlife nicely preserved in toxic black muck. Luckily our neighbours, the Corkums, had a better well, primly jacketed in concrete and open to the light so you could check for drowned varmints, and somehow Mum prevailed upon the grumpy old couple to allow us to use it, although I never mastered the special gentle way of dropping the bucket that Mrs. Corkum prescribed and spent long periods under banishment. The Corkums' well never ran dry, although in the summer when it got low it developed another issue common to coastal wells: it became infiltrated with seawater. I still remember the seaweedy taste that crept into everything and utterly defeated the use of soap.

When Dad built our new house at Kent Road he dug a well in the low, swampy side of the property. Swamp wells were not considered the best but they did tend to keep going in dry weather and this one was in the same swamp as the well used by the Patons, who didn't seem to have the blind staggers, so my dad chanced it. For ten months of a year it was brimming with somewhat drinkable water that had a distinctive tang reminiscent of skunk cabbage, but during the fall and spring and winter and early summer rainy seasons it overflowed and mixed with the sludgy water from the Kent Road ditch, which wasn't good. This didn't stop it from dwindling in the driest months to the point you could only collect a teacupful at a time. Dad always took this as a signal to go deeper, and one of my punishments was to log long summer hours down that well miserably chipping away at the marble-like hardpan with a spike bar, feeling like some medieval lifer trying to chip his way out of a dungeon. At least it was cool.

Eventually we wore that hole down far enough to stay wet during the driest summer and even suited it up with a nice casing of concrete complete with a varmint-proof cover and an electric pressure pump that supplied our home with that greatest of all mod cons, running water. Still, the pump needed constant doctoring and replacing and every summer still meant going on short water rations. You got a thump on the noggin if you rinsed your toothbrush under a running tap instead of using a small, partly filled glass. Anybody who grew up around here during those times became a water conservationist out of necessity. Not only was bathwater saved for the garden, you only filled the tub once a week and every member of the family took turns in the same increasingly soupy load, working from smallest to largest. Only then did Mum ladle it into little thumb-holes beside each bean plant. We would just about faint if we saw some city dweller wash a spud under a running tap, take a fifteen-minute shower, or horror of horrors, water grass with a sprinkler.

When old Colonel Johnstone and Rod Webb came around signing people up to form the South Pender Water Improvement District to pipe water down from Haslam Lake, my dad signed eagerly. After that the old habit of treating potable water as something to be doled out like single malt slowly fell away and we joined the modern world in regarding it as being as expendable as air.

Too bad. Very large parts of North America, especially the parts that victual our dinner tables, are on the verge of the greatest water shortage since the creation of the Sahara. Oil-well technology is being employed in a desperate search for deeper aquifers, planners are studying trillion-dollar schemes for rerouting rivers, and every year parched Americans gaze more thirstily at Canada's brimming lakes and streams. But too few are looking for water in the most obvious place: curbing wasteful use. Just running the tap while brushing your teeth wastes three thousand gallons a year. If we could only get all five hundred million North Americans to adopt the mild conservation measures recommended by the EPA (low-flow showerheads, two-stage toilets, fixing drippy taps, etc.) the effect would be like discovering another Lake Superior.

And nobody would have to go sharesies in the bathtub to do it. Unless they wanted to, of course.

Restricted Visibility

A few days ago I got a little reminder that it was once again time for me to drop by the ICBC office in Sechelt to renew my driver's licence. I of course left it until the last day, wanting to squeeze the last drop of goodness out of my old licence, and found the renewal wonderfully trivial. This was due mainly to the sweet ministrations of the lady who guides you through the process and takes your new (hatless, glassless, unsmiling) photo and who has the most amazing makeup job this side of Boy George, complete with glitter lip paint that is a work of art in itself. Obviously doing what she can do to brighten up a dull corner of our lives, and I for one appreciate it.

Along the way I got counting the number of times I've made this particular little journey and figured it must be number ten—not counting the actual getting of the licence on the very day of my sixteenth birthday in 1961, which was certainly the most memorable trip of the bunch. Nowadays it takes three years of tests and L-plates and N-plates to get a driver's licence—if you can afford the high-risk insurance—but in those days a kid could take his written test and do his road test and walk away with a full-bore licence on day one.

Not only that, I took mine in my dad's gravel truck and became an instant commercial truck driver. I was eager to get launched on my driving career like any kid, but my dad was even more eager. For years he'd been using me as an unpaid swamper in his one-man sand and gravel business and he couldn't wait to get me hauling dirt legally. I think I delivered my first load of pit-run later the same day. I guess I must have driven half a million miles since, in a variety of vehicles ranging from motor scooters to off-road earth movers in all parts of Canada and other places where they still drive on the wrong side of the road.

By far the majority of those miles have been piled up looping up and down our own Sunshine Coast Highway and it occurred to me on the way back home this has become how I know this place.

The generation just before mine navigated the territory mainly by boat and when they dozed off in their dotage years dreaming of the place they'd spent their days must have pictured a completely different landscape from the one I know—one of islands, harbours and red-railinged government wharves. My Sunshine Coast has been a long string of hills and curves and roadside scenes known only by momentary glimpses from a speeding vehicle.

When I doze off I won't be picturing the world-famous facade of Molly's Reach but the funny little shake cottage on North Road with the knick-knacks in the window. You know the one. It's the kind of window you only see trimmed with snow on old-time Christmas cards now, a window checkered into panes the size of a child's face, and for years each pane in that cottage had a little novelty perching in it—a twirling crystal or a miniature teacup or an origami bird—it was hard to tell exactly what from a whizzing car but the display endured for decades, cheering me each time I passed. I often wished I had the nerve to pull into the bushy little driveway and thank the person for brightening up another dull corner of life but I never did and lately I've noticed that although the cabin remains, the knick-knacks are gone. I'm sure there's a sad story behind that but it was a truly amazing run.

Then there are sadder landmarks—one a thick maple on North Road just above the hairpin and another stout cedar just north of Wakefield, both with bark missing where friends of mine ploughed into them at speed, doing far more harm to themselves than the trees. I see they have cut down the cedar, which had broken many lives—although it would be more helpful if they fixed the road. In fifty-five years you unfortunately get to know a lot of corners that way—this is where Mike Klein bought it, this where Cathy and Josh ended their journey, this where little Sam went into the icy water and never came out.

I always knock ten k off my speed and go on high alert on the section of highway that circles Trout Lake because I have seen so much mayhem there, with probably more fatalities than any other half-mile stretch on the coast, except possibly Rat Portage Hill, where my wife had her nice little Mini head-oned. When I was in the business of hauling van loads of peanut hockey players they liked to yell "Go faster!" whenever they noticed me pussyfooting around Trout Lake, so I explained to them that it was accursed ground where bad spirits lurked ready to pull unwary drivers into the water like those rock monsters in the Nissan ad. They hooted disbelief, but I like to think they paid attention on some level because to date none of them have fallen prey to the monsters.

A few times I have had the pleasure of flying over the Sunshine Coast and have been surprised at how unfamiliar everything looks when you see the whole of it. I keep peering down wondering just where the heck that is, and find myself locating everything by where it would be on the road—that must be Davis Bay, the one truly scenic break on the scenic Sunshine Coast Highway; that must be the straight stretch above Norwest Bay hill—who knew there were so many houses tucked into the bush around there? It makes you realize how little we really know this place we think we know so well, and I always resolve that when I get back to earth I'll get off the beaten path and do some belated exploring of the hinterlands. But then I get strapped in that familiar old driver's seat and forget all about it. I think there is a metaphor about life hidden somewhere here.

Munga's Meadows

There are some improvements that come to one after getting past the regulation threescore and ten and starting to bite into overtime. Not many, but some. One is that it is harder to keep putting things off. Munga, my dear old dad, once took a Sunday off while logging the lower slopes of Mount Garibaldi to climb up to the alpine meadows and surmount the Black Tusk. Some of my earliest memories are of him effusing about the ocean of wildflowers to be seen up there. At five, and no less at fifteen, wildflowers, even oceans of them, were not among my top ten interests, but I was impressed by how much my unflowery dad was impressed by them, and how much he wanted to get us kids up there to see them at the first chance. "You just wouldn't believe it until you see it," he kept exclaiming down through the decades.

He went into double and triple overtime before dying at 101 but never managed to deliver on his tantalizing promise to show us the unbelievable ocean of Garibaldi flowers, leaving me to carry the ambition along in my own life, putting it off through the growing up of my own children and now half through that of my grandchildren. But even in the thickest skulls some light dawns at last, and when my nephew Doug spoke of taking his kids—Martin, five, and Sophie, ten—along with my two granddaughters Simone and Eloise on an alpine jaunt some summer, I

jumped in and said, "Okay, let's actually do that, and right now."
So it happened.

Instead of Garibaldi, which these days is so crammed with
flower sniffers you have to reserve ahead to merely get on the
trail, Doug chose Manning Park, which promised equally vast
meadows also within reach of preschoolers and geriatrics. The
Heather Trail at Manning, though devoid of heather, has the
advantage of a good road up to the six-thousand-foot level, so
you're into the alpine as soon as you leave the parking lot. My
type of mountaineering.

The idea of course was to expose these young minds to the
wonder that is nature, so that they might find, as the famous
naturalist Rachel Carson wrote, in "the beauty of the earth …
reserves of strength that will endure as long as life lasts."

Results were mixed. The alpine flowers, stretching as far as
the eye could see, were much enjoyed by the adults but pro-
voked only sit-down strikes by the younger hikers, not because
backpacking through the unending brilliance was too exhaust-
ing, but because "*This is so boring!*" The wonders that are whisky
jacks saved us the first day, with their nervy willingness to snap
Cheerios out of children's fingers even after repeated attempts
to imprison them under ball caps. Succeeding campsites had no
whisky jacks, but were riddled with the burrows of ground squirrels, which the kids made frenzied efforts to capture by pouring
cups of water down the supposed entry holes while posting sen-
tries at the supposed exit holes. Making an accurate estimate of
their chances of success, we cynically promised that they could
take home any squirrels they caught, which drove them to even
more frenzied pouring and digging and led to bloody rebellion
when we insisted on leaving squirrel-less the next morning.

On the way home we bought a seventy-six dollar space at a
drive-in campsite with flush toilets, massive RVs and kids whizzing around on barking mini-bikes. We adults were appalled by

the bustle and din and conspicuous display of heavy-duty camping fixtures but the kids seemed relieved to be back in civilized surroundings with Wi-Fi and amused themselves by playing house in my decrepit Toyota Matrix. In fact they were having such shrieking good fun we let them get their sleeping bags and spend the night there on the promise they wouldn't shriek all night, which promise they sort of kept.

When I asked them at the end of the week what the highlight of the trip was they replied in unison—you guessed it—"that night you let us sleep in the car!" The wonder that is nature rated no mention. But at least I got to see the ocean of wildflowers, and to finally appreciate what my dad had been talking about all those years ago. Sometimes a parent's influence just takes a while to sink in.

Shadows in Our Sunshine

Sometimes I think about the people I have known on the Sunshine Coast and try to imagine which one I'd pick if I were given the job of selecting one to be on our flag or serve as our human mascot the way the little finger-in-the-dike boy does in Holland, or the broken-note-bugler does for Krakow. There is such a tempting bouquet of character to choose from—but today I am thinking of one of my absolute favourites, Hubert Evans.

Hubert moved to Roberts Creek in 1928, following overseas service in WW I and stints as a newspaperman in Nelson and New Westminster. He was launched on a career that seemed to be pointing straight up—meaning straight to Toronto—when he suddenly pulled the plug and moved his young family to a bare piece of land on what was then a very isolated part of the BC coast. In the local history book *Remembering Roberts Creek* he wrote about the epiphany that turned his career around and made him a coast lifer:

In April 1927 a young couple seeking a less hurried life-style than they had found in cities visited Roberts Creek. During a stroll they stopped to watch an elderly man fastening claws to the end of a long cedar pole he had shaped.

"For hooking up mussels, the big ones down low on the wharf piles," the man explained.

"Mussels for eating?"

"For catching shiners tomorrow. Shiners make good cod bait. I aim to go cod fishing the day after."

Three unhurried days to catch a cod! Then and there the couple knew their search had ended.

I think it wasn't just the leisure aspect of this vision of coastal life that appealed to Hubert but the artfulness. He delighted in mastering practical detail, in getting things like catching codfish right, and in reducing the hurly-burly of modern life to simple concrete tasks. He beachcombed the logs that he used to make the lumber for his sturdy clapboard cottage, which still stands. When latter-day visitors stooped to admire his edge-grain fir flooring, he would describe how it came from a fine fir peeler he spotted drifting by one day and towed to Roberts' mill with his rowboat, his delight at the find—and at the self-sufficiency afforded by coastal life in those days—undiminished by the sixty seasons that had passed.

Upon first arriving, Hubert supported the family by writing stories for pulp magazines but when the dirty thirties dried up markets he was forced to turn fisherman. He entered the trade like a lot of hard-up breadwinners in those days—by dragging a single handline behind his rowboat. There were enough fish then you could make a dollar or two on a good day, and failing that you could always hook something to eat. There was a considerable fleet of handliners chasing coho over at Poor Man's Rock and he set about learning the fine points of the fishing trade in his usual workmanlike way.

One result was an elegant double-ended trolling skiff, which he lovingly crafted with his own hands during the off-season. It was such a fine example of the type it is now the pride of the Sunshine Coast Museum in Gibsons, testament to a time when even successful professionals were forced to roll up their sleeves and support their families with the labour of their own hands.

Hubert was one of those who thought the Great Depression had taught his generation an essential lesson about getting back to basics and also about the need for humane values in government, lessons he felt we are in danger of losing the more those hard times fade into memory. During WW II Hubert did his part by writing thoughtful stories designed to make people think beyond the jingoism of the time. One fine example was a serialized novella called *No More Islands* which examined the internment of the Japanese residents of a coastal community recognizable as our own Sunshine Coast. The story still sizzles, not only because of its vivid description of the unnecessary cruelty visited upon local pioneers of Japanese descent, but also because of its evocation of the 9/11-like hysteria that incited many of their non-Japanese neighbours to support such treatment.

Hubert's undeniable masterpiece was his novel *Mist on the River*, based on a stint he did as an aid worker among Gitksan–Wet'suwet'en villages on the Skeena during the 1950s. It has a place in literary history as the first Canadian novel to depict First Nations realistically as central characters, and is still relevant enough that a group of Indigenous filmmakers are determined to develop it as a feature film.

CanLit icon Margaret Laurence called Hubert "the elder of our tribe" and visited the coast to help SFU award him an honorary doctorate, the only time the university had seen fit to award a doctorate in a private home. Every year in Vancouver or Victoria the Hubert Evans Prize is awarded to the writer of the best non-fiction book in BC, but here on his home turf nothing remains to mark his name. That seems a shame for one of our more distinguished pioneers, a man who understood us well enough to write this little verse called "Coast People":

> *So here we are, the lot of us—*
> *Pilgrims and profligates*
> *Builders and upsetters of applecarts*
> *Dispossessed and dispossessors.*
> *Which have found the life they hoped to find?*
> *Which have shadows in their sunshine still?*

Amen.

ACKNOWLEDGMENTS

Many earlier and usually less rambling versions of these sketches were published in the excellent regional magazine *Coast Life*. My thanks to editors John Snelgrove, Shelley Ambrose and Jan DeGrass for their patient prodding over the years. Others may seem like they were previously published but that is only because I have an unfortunate habit of repeating myself without realizing it. When you've lived in the same tiny town for sixty-five years life itself sometimes begins to seem like it's repeating itself.

Before I go I would like to acknowledge Roderick Barman for his extraordinary insight and generosity in providing us with the perfect cover image. Dr. Barman spotted that beautiful W.J. Phillips woodcut in a gallery catalogue last summer and brought it to my attention, having noticed it was labelled as a scene from Pender Harbour, my hometown. What he did not know was that it was a view from the exact property where I lived as a kid and featured the rickety little dock where my sisters and I had spent many of our most memorable days. We had long been intrigued that a famous artist had found his way to that obscure notch of the BC coastline only a few months before we moved there and had captured our very personal little scene for posterity, but I never expected to have an original copy of the print in my possession. Once Roderick discovered that special connection, he made sure that the print found its way into my hands. He said he wanted to show gratitude for my efforts on behalf of British Columbia publishing and literature over the years. I do sometimes have doubts about how I have spent those years, and it helps very much to look up at that lovely print where it hangs on the wall above my desk. Thank you, Roderick.